Nostalgic
Wolverhampton

Part of the
Memories
series

THE PUBLISHERS WOULD LIKE TO THANK THE FOLLOWING
COMPANIES FOR SUPPORTING THE PRODUCTION OF THIS BOOK

BEACON CENTRE FOR THE BLIND

CD BRAMALL WOLVERHAMPTON

CAROL'S MOTORS LIMITED (WOLVERHAMPTON)

COMPTON HOSPICE

CHUBB SAFE EQUIPMENT COMPANY

SJ DIXON

FA GILL LIMITED

ARTHUR M GRIFFITHS & SON LIMITED

HUGHES & HOLMES LIMITED

IMI WOLVERHAMPTON METAL LIMITED

JARVIS MOUNT HOTEL

F JENNINGS & SONS LIMITED

MANBY STEWARD SOLICITORS

MANDER BROTHERS LIMITED

THE MANDER CENTRE

MURAS BAKER JONES & CO

J POTTS & SON

ROYAL ORDNANCE SPECIALITY METALS

THE ROYAL WOLVERHAMPTON SCHOOL

J RUDELL & COMPANY

SANDERS, WRIGHT & FREEMAN

THE WULFRUN CENTRE

First published in Great Britain by True North Books Limited
Units 3 - 5 Heathfield Industrial Park
Elland West Yorkshire
HX5 9AE
Tel. 01422 377977
© Copyright: True North Books Limited 1999

ISBN 1 900463 53 9

Text, design and origination by True North Books Limited, Elland, West Yorkshire
Printed and bound by The Amadeus Press Limited, Huddersfield, West Yorkshire

Memories are made of this

Memories. We all have them; some good, some bad, but our memories of the town we grew up in are usually tucked away in a very special place in our minds. The best are usually connected with our childhood and youth, when we longed to be grown up and paid no attention to adults who told us to enjoy our youth, as these were the best years of our lives. We look back now and realise that they were right.

Some of us remember the wonderful parties that

were held to celebrate the coronation in 1953. Others remember the nights spent jiving at the Queen's Ballroom, queuing up before the doors opened in a long line that stretched around the building. We remember shopping for our trendy gear at the Top Twenty fashion shop, buying our first records at the Voltic in the Queen's Arcade, and congregating at the Milano coffee bar in Darlington Street with our mates.

So many memories. And so many changes. Wolverhampton in the 1960s before the Mander and Wulfrun Centres were built, and the main shopping streets were pedestrianised. What a

difference it made not to have to take your life in your hands just to cross Dudley Street to browse around Woolworths or C&A!

And we can think of sweeping changes of a different kind, when new trends in shopping led to the very first self-serve stores being opened. How strange it felt at first to pick up a basket (those were the days before shopping trolleys!) and help ourselves from the goods on display on the shelves - it was almost like stealing! The trend led eventually to out-of-town shopping in centres such as Merry Hill.

Through the bad times and the good, however, Wolverhampton not only survived but prospered. We have only to compare the town as it is today with its new shopping centres and up-to-the-minute facilities with the town as it was, say in the 1940s, to see what progress has been realised and what achievements have been made over the last 50 years. Wolverhampton has a history to be proud of - but more importantly, a great future to look forward to, into the new millennium and beyond.

Contents

Around the town centre

Situated on the corner of Lichfield Street, the Criterion Hotel was during the 1930s a thriving town centre pub, though during the next 30 years the establishment was to become rather notorious. The pub eventually closed and the building was taken over by the university, and today the old Criterion is put to a different use, housing the Higher Education 'shop' where students can choose and discuss their courses.

Almost within view on the right of Lichfield Street is the Grand Theatre, the scene of many pleasant memories that go right back to the days when we shouted 'He's behind you!' and responded to the inevitable 'Oh no he isn't' with 'Oh yes he is!' We all enjoyed the pantomime: Cinderella and Buttons, the fairy godmother, the ugly sisters and, of course, the prince, complete with shapely legs and high heels. But the Grand has provided us with more than panto, staging variety shows, plays, musical comedy and Gilbert & Sullivan, and welcoming well-known entertainers such as the celebrated Marlene Dietrich. The theatre closed at the end of 1979, and the local supporters' group swung into action to save the Grand. In 1983 the wonderful old theatre did reopen, and has recently gone through extensive restorations.

Above: An extraordinary number of fine old cars are to be seen in this view of Queen Square, taking into account the fact that it was taken during World War II. Several vehicles are driving through the Square, while half a dozen more are parked in Lychgate. Though there were a good number of private cars on the road at the time, petrol rationing, introduced in September 1939, severely curtailed the length of their journeys, and the vast majority of ordinary people travelled by public transport. The enormous 'Players Please Everyone' sign on the wall of the tobacconists Salmon & Gluckstein was once a familiar sight in Queen Square; smoking was not at that time seen to pose any threat to health and non-smokers were very much in the minority. The plinth of Prince Albert's statue is here being used not only to provide a seat for a tired elderly lady but to encourage people to buy National Savings Certificates: 'Money talks, let your's shout victory' declares the bold sign. Across the road a prominent sign outside Barclays bank invites passers-by to buy National War Bonds. Unadorned by the bushes that once discreetly screened the facilities (and would again in future years), the public conveniences lie beneath the prince's stony gaze.

Above right: The impressive Royal London Insurance building dominates this 1930s view of Prince's Square, though perhaps the detail that is likely to catch our eye is the unusual set of traffic

lights set slap bang in the centre of the square. Prince's Square was privileged to have the first set of traffic lights in England installed in 1928, and the newspaper proudly pointed out that Wolverhampton was 'ahead of other towns with automatic signals.' Even the city of Birmingham had none. Those first lights were suspended rather than being mounted on a pole, and when they were first installed (and for some time afterwards), drivers who were strangers to the town were confused as to the procedure. The Birmingham man who was fined £1 for running a red light must have complained bitterly, though he would have been told that ignorance of the law was no excuse. Among the businesses that had their blinds up on that sunny day long ago was W Snape, whose tea and coffee shop was legendary in the town. Snapes still have a thriving business in Queen Street, where discerning customers can have tea weighed out in the traditional way.

The Darlington Street of 1900 betrays nothing of the frenzied haste and hurry that was to characterise this same stretch of road 100 years on. Pictured in the days when noise from the town's traffic involved only the rattle of wheels and the trotting of hooves, the only traffic pollution here could be put to good use on the land! Straight as a draughtsman's rule, Darlington Street was laid out in 1821 on land acquired by the town from Lord Darlington. The horse-drawn open-topped tram may look romantic and full of character, but a journey on those early trams was hardly a luxury ride.

They had uncomfortable wooden slat seats and straw scattered on the floor, and a couple of oil lamps gave out what light they could. A less than pleasant ride in a typical British winter! The horse-drawn tram had nearly had its day, though, as electric trams took over in 1902 - and motor buses were introduced in 1904.
St Marks church (built after Darlington Street had been laid out) stands like a sentinel at the junction with Salop Street in Chapel Ash, while on the right smoke drifts from the tall chimney of the Park Brewery. The Ring Road Island today occupies much of this area.

This is almost like one of those 'spot the deliberate error' pictures, only this time it's 'spot the missing dome'! In the early years of the 20th century the roof of the Midland Bank building boasted not only an elegant little tower capped with a shapely dome, but also a time ball mounted above the dome. Fire caused both to be removed, but in recent years a dome has once more been added to the building. The Cafe Royal is a name that will bring back many happy memories to readers who frequented the popular upmarket cafe in their younger days. And who remembers the Queens Cinema, in the background on the right?

In 1959 it became the Queens Ballroom; those were the days of jive, and on Club Nights a long queue would form outside long before the doors opened. In 1980 the ballroom was demolished to make way for Lloyds Bank. Queen Square boasted a number of banks; Martins Bank can be seen in the left foreground, with Barclays further along on the same side of the road. The square was redesigned in 1951 to celebrate the Festival of Britain; the statue of Prince Albert was moved further down the road, and a garden was planted above the public conveniences. During the 1990s Queen Square was pedestrianised.

Bottom: A tranquil view of St Peter's church, showing the town's ancient Saxon Cross on the far right. The war memorial on the left honours the names of those who gave their lives in the two world wars. Note that the open market still occupied its traditional place in the shadow of the church in this photograph, though its actual date is unknown; the frontage of the church has gone through a major facelift since then. The new markets were newer and smarter, but the energetic atmosphere of the old, the aromas of its fruit and vegetables and its flower stalls, and the cheerful shouts of its traders is still sadly missed by many. Perhaps 'the old days' acquire a kind of 'golden glow' as time passes, and our nostalgia makes us forget the many improvements that have been made since then?

Giffard House, where back in the 17th century its brave Roman Catholic owner broke the law by worshipping in his own chapel, can be seen in the background. To the right of the house you might be able to pick out the chimneys of Goodyear Tyres. More than a few readers will have been among the crowd of hundreds who came to view their end. No Fred Dibnah fire-lighting methods here; the chimneys were blown up with explosives.

Right: This view of Queen Square in 1950 reveals a fascinating spiders' web of trolley wires. Single-deck 36-passenger 'trackless trams' began running between Wolverhampton and Wednesfield as early as 1923, running in conjunction with the motor bus service that took over from trams in the early years of the century. Wolverhampton's trolley bus system was to go down in history as the largest in the world. By the 1960s, however, there was a certain amount of murmuring about the overhead electric wires that looked ugly and restricted buses to prescribed routes, and the Transport Committee came down on the side of diesel-engined buses. The last trolley bus ran on 5th March 1967. Public transport was to come full circle in the 1990s when tramlines were laid once more in Wolverhampton. The pedestrians seen here are all appear to be walking briskly and purposefully (apart from the man on the far right who is engaged in taking a photograph), which would suggest that this was the normal teatime rush to get home from work at the end of the day. At the time the Tudor-style building on the left was the Shakespeare pub, an Atkinson's house.

Above: The palatial Bank of England building provides the stately backdrop for this view of Queen Square, taken around 1950. A clock in the distance informs us that it is 5pm, so these busy pedestrians will no doubt be making their way home from work or from the shops. Outside the door of the bank a mother pushes a large coach-built pram; unless her home is not too far from the centre, we wonder how she managed to bring it so far. She would certainly not be able to get it on the bus! These were rather ignominious days for Prince Albert, whose statue gazes down impassively at the public toilets and the traders' carts parked nearby - a far cry from those heady days of glory, when in 1866 Queen Victoria came out of mourning to unveil her consort's statue. Nobody imagined that she would accept the invitation, and when she unexpectedly agreed to visit Wolverhampton the whole town went into a spin. In only nine days the town was transformed into a riot of red, white and blue as flags and garlands were hung from every available lamp post. The occasion held another surprise, as during the unveiling ceremony the Queen unexpectedly borrowed a sword and knighted the Mayor.

Top: This 1940s photograph of Prince's Square is very typical of the day, from the fashions and hairstyles of the young girls waiting to cross Lichfield Street at the traffic island to the 'Please Cross Here' signs on the bollards. The motor cyclist about to turn the corner by the Westminster Bank in the centre of the picture also betrays the attitude of the day - back then it was quite legal to ride without a helmet. The number of traffic signs would appear rather confusing, though in the 40s you were unlikely to become a victim of road rage if you slowed down to take a closer look - then changed your mind about which direction you should take. The instruction 'Move only on green' was an attempt to stop 'amber gamblers' from racing away before the green light appeared. This section of Lichfield Street all the way to Queen Square (off to the right of the photograph) has now, of course, been pedestrianised. Though today's traffic is much heavier than it was in the 1940s, pedestrianised areas and one-way systems have made the town centre a far safer place for people. The Ring Road has done a superb job of keeping through traffic away from the once-congested town centre.

Have you ever noticed how large the cars of the 1920s and 30s were in comparison with today's compact motors? Economy driving does not relate to this line of parked vehicles in Queen Square! The wonderful old Lyons van on the left brings to mind a certain vehicle from 'Dad's Army'....

The streets are crowded with pedestrians as well as parked cars in this 1930s view of the square, and the fact that the pavement outside Lyons Restaurant on the far left is packed with would-be diners would indicate that the photograph was taken one lunch time. The mock-Tudor Shakespeare pub with its

well-known pediments would one day become the premises of the M & B jeweller's. Readers will recognise the white building in the distance as Burton's tailors, which in 1992 was taken over and incorporated into the adjacent Beatties department store. The public conveniences in Queen Square have an interesting history. Built in 1902 for visitors to the Art and Industrial Exhibition, they were among the first in the country to provide facilities for ladies as well as men; the toilets were at that time screened behind bushes - no respectable lady would want anyone to see where she was going!

Above: A wonderfully evocative photograph of Lichfield Street from Prince's Square in the 1930s, when traffic lights were still a novelty in the town. The sign above the shop on the left tell us that this belonged to the London Midland & Scottish Railway, and a beautiful countryside view occupies much of the window, enticing the passer-by to book a Frames railway tour. Note the sign over the door offering an interesting service: 'Parcels received and forwarded'. The shop next door was United Talking Machines, where for only five shillings a week you could take home a 'His Master's Voice' radio or gramophone. The HMV logo is one of the 20th Century's most well known trademarks. The small dog in their advert was Nipper, whose master, the English artist Francis Barraud, painted him alongside a gramophone he borrowed from the Gramophone Company. The company eventually bought the picture and adopted it as their trademark.

A notice below the traffic lights, which are interestingly positioned in the centre of the square, advises motorists somewhat confusingly 'Turning right keep right'. Much of this area is today dedicated to education, and the University School of Health Science occupies premises on the right that once housed the main Post Office.

IN THE 1930s FOR JUST FIVE SHILLINGS A WEEK YOU COULD TAKE HOME A HMV RADIO OR GRAMOPHONE

Right: This wonder-  fully ornate lamp standard with its four lamps and decorative curlicues deserves a mention in its own right. The standard once graced the Snow Hill and Cleveland Street roundabout, though goodness help any motorist unfamiliar with the roads who suddenly found himself faced with this busy forest of traffic signs! Two signs instruct him to go left to Bridgnorth, Shrewsbury, Chester and North Wales, while if he wants to go to the centre or to Stafford he should go straight on. A right turn will take him to West Bromwich, Birmingham, Cannock and Stafford. The largest sign of all directs him to keep left, an instruction which seems to hardly warrant a sign of this size. As far as the eye can see, however, as we look towards the bottom of Dudley Street, the roads appear to be totally deserted of traffic, and there are more pedestrians than cars about. The businesses trading here at the time might evoke a few memories; Barclays Bank, C D Nokes at numbers 55-56; the tobacconist next door advertises Wills Gold Flake, and Ling's Music Stores is further along; occupying a prime position on the right was Billingham's, who were the authorised Ford dealers.

Below: One-way traffic is a relatively recent development in Salop Street; during the 1940s vehicles could not only travel in either direction but they could also park on both sides of the road! A notice beneath the traffic lights tells motorists to 'move only on green' - an instruction we find confusing until we find out that this photograph was taken during an experiment in omitting the red-amber sequence to try to stop drivers setting off before the lights changed to green. The block on the right was built in 1927, and H Cohen's outfitters (today the Red House fashions) occupied a prime position on the corner. On the left of the photograph is a branch of Edwin Blakemore's grocery stores; there were several branches in Wolverhampton. They were coffee blenders and roasters, and the aroma of roasting coffee must have been very enticing. Ovaltine and Bovril are among the products advertised in Blakemore's window; lovers of trivia might like to know that the catch-phrase 'Bovril prevents that sinking feeling' was designed before World War I but was withheld at the time as a mark of respect for the families of those lost on the 'Titanic'.

Above: This atmospheric photograph of Lichfield Street in the 1930s shows us how little this stretch of road has changed over the years - except, that is, for the presence of traffic. A second look will tell us that most of the vehicles pictured here are public transport rather than private cars; the days when most families would own at least one car were then still in the far distant future. If you wanted to go anywhere, whether it was into town to do some shopping or a Saturday evening visit to the cinema, you went by bus. The Art Gallery and Museum has changed little if at all, though the gardens have been redesigned again and again over the years. The railings that once surrounded the gardens were removed during World War II as part of the war effort, but recent restoration work has added railings to the garden once more - a nice touch. In the distance the Royal London Insurance building can just be picked out; one of the businesses housed in the building was a tailor whose claim to fame was that he made suits for the well-known actor and comedian Norman Wisdom!

Do you remember Victoria Street before the Mander Centre? Remember the Maypole Dairy, where many of us bought our groceries in days gone by? Nobody gave those rather nice lamps hanging above the window a second glance back in 1950, when this photograph was taken; perhaps it takes a few decades for us to appreciate what we once took for granted! And what about Adrien's? They were acknowledged as the place to shop, and the very sparseness of Adrien's classy window display emphasised their exclusive fashions that were beyond the pocket of all but the more affluent Wulfrunians. This row of properties, built in 1906, has gone now, of course. Beatties has changed little apart from extending in 1992 to incorporate the Burtons building on the corner of Darlington Street (note the art-deco elephants above the upper windows). It was back in 1877 that James Beattie founded the Victoria Drapery Stores in Victoria Street, and from that small beginning sprang the successful town-centre department store. Beatties' extended in 1960 into the adjoining premises of F W Bradford & Son and Jeanette's fashions. Note the pedestrian crossing in the foreground; it's interesting to note that although Belisha beacons are in place here, zebra lines have not yet been introduced.

Above: Dudley Street in 1960, and the Irish Linen Depot on the corner of King Street was still able to rate itself as 'The linen cupboard of Wolverhampton'. Dunns gents outfitters occupied the opposite corner premises at that time; Dunns were at one time exclusively hatters, but as styles changed and the wearing of hats was not such a fashion statement as it had been in the 1930s and 40s, the well-known chain extended their services to general men's outfitting. The building still stands, though Dunns no longer have these shop premises; the Irish Linen Depot was demolished. A 'No Entry' sign guards the end of King Street from intruding traffic, but one enterprising lady is determined to get around this problem by pushing her bike instead of riding it, thereby becoming a pedestrian rather than a rider. By the early 1960s Dudley Street was becoming congested with traffic, and 'No Waiting' signs warn drivers off parking at the kerb. The area was to see major developments in the years ahead, with pedestrianisation banning the car from Dudley Street, the building of the revolutionary new C & A store, and the modern Dudley Street branch of Woolworths which was to be the largest in Europe.

Below: Isn't it amazing how familiarity can breed, if not contempt, at least inattention? Passers-by in Lichfield Street are obviously so used to seeing the Art Gallery that they rarely if ever stop to admire the beautiful Italian-style building, which is now more than 100 years old. The left edge of the photograph almost but not quite captures the Horsman Fountain, built to honour Philip Horsman, whose generous donation gave the Art Gallery to Wolverhampton. Built from granite and Portland Stone, the fountain's cupids, dolphins and cascading water have delighted Wulfrunians since it was unveiled in May 1896. A web of trolley-bus lines above indicates the public transport system that was in use at the time; the trolley on the left carries an advertisement for Littlewoods football pools. Long before the National Lottery made people think that 'it might be them', Littlewoods and Vernons offered people a chance to strike it lucky by 'doing the pools' every week. Children were shushed into silence while those all-important results were read out over the radio - and more often than not it was a case of 'no luck again this week'.

Below: Once marked by its inferior housing, Lichfield Street had by the early years of the 20th century become an impressive example of shops and business premises. An anonymous donation of £5,000 - incredibly generous for the time - paid for the Art Gallery and Museum on the left.

The identity of the donor was later discovered and was found to be a local builder, Philip Horsman. The building was designed by Birmingham architect Julius Chatwin in the Italianate-style, and it was built by Horsman's own company. The Gallery opened in 1884.

THE ART GALLERY AND MUSEUM WAS PAID FOR BY A DONATION BY A LOCAL BUILDER, PHILIP HORSMAN

The Horsman Fountain in the left foreground commemorates his generous act.

This photograph dates from the mid-1950s, and though the names above the shop windows have changed, many readers will remember this stretch of Lichfield Street as it was when Repairwell, Sketchley Dry Cleaning and James Baker & Sons occupied some of these properties on the left. In the Midland Bank next to the Art Gallery, the clink of glasses and the buzz of conversation is more likely to be heard today than the quiet rustle of banknotes being counted.

Below: One of the first things to catch the eye in this busy view of Queen Street is, of course, that the cars lining the kerbside are facing in both directions. Today Queen Street is part of Wolverhampton's one-way system that keeps town centre traffic flowing relatively smoothly, but which visitors to the town can find confusing. A Number 43 motor bus bound for Castlecroft is passing the impressive classical facade of what was then the County Court. Diesel engined motor buses began to replace the old trolley bus system in 1961, and one by one the trolley routes disappeared and gave way to the buses. The number 58 Dudley via Sedgley was the last route to be replaced; it went on March 5th 1967.

In the distance readers with a sharp eye will be able to pick out the entrance to High Level Station; originally the High Level was on the LMS (London Midland & Scottish Railway) line, while the Low Level station belonged to the GWR (Great Western Railway). In 1963 the two rival lines were made part of the London Midland Region.

The County Court on the right of the photograph is better known to the younger generation of Wulfrunians as Chancellor's bistro.

Right: This fascinating view of Queen Square was shot in 1964. Banks and building societies are often given scant attention from passers-by who hurriedly call in to pay a bill, make a deposit or use the cash machine; given a second glance, however, they are usually among the architecturally more interesting buildings in any town. Barclays Bank, the back of which can be seen on the left, is a good example of a building that deserves more than a passing glance. Lady readers will remember shopping at Joans fashions, facing the side of the bank across Lychgate. The interesting Tudor-style building across the square is M & B Jewellers, which in earlier years was The Shakespeare public house. To its left is J Lyons & Co Ltd and to its right, Reynolds Restaurant, where Wulfrunians spent many a happy hour over coffee and buttered scones, or enjoyed a more substantial meal. The chimney of the Manders printing ink factory stands tall behind Queen Square; today the view is very different, with the Mander Shopping Centre occupying the place where many of these properties used to stand. St John's church spire, surrounded by contractors' scaffolding, juts into the skyline.

Which clock is telling the right time? The photograph reveals an interesting situation: the clock above M & B Jewellers, advertising 'watches of Switzerland' reads 12.40, while the neighbouring clock mounted on the walls of the rather pukka Reynolds Restaurant disagrees, arguing that the time is 12.46. Whatever the time, though, it is still lunch time and the two girls standing near the bench are hungry enough to be enjoying an outdoor snack.

A queue has formed at the Tettenhall bus stop, and the number of heavy shopping baskets that have been placed on the pavement leads us to conclude that these are mostly shoppers returning home after a busy Saturday morning around the town centre stores. A trolley bus is just about to pass Prince Albert's statue, the trolley together with the cars and the fashions worn by passers-by help us to date this photograph to the 1960s, when trolley buses were still a familiar sight around the town. Trolley buses were introduced to Wolverhampton in 1923, and the popular 'trackless tram' system was to last for 44 years before being totally replaced by diesel buses. In the distance can be seen the distinctive Burton building that was typical of Burton's men's outfitters just about everywhere; the building was later taken over by Beatties.

Below: Pedestrians wait on the roundabout to cross Broad Street, traditionally busy with heavy traffic. The roundabout disappeared in the name of progress; what happened to the remarkable clock-on-a-pole that once stood there? The ever-popular Morris Minor in the centre of the photograph will bring back many fond memories among readers who remember its brilliant cornering and steering qualities; designed by Sir Alexander Issigonis in the late 1940s the car became the first all-British car to sell more than one million, and it remained in production until 1971.

On the left of the photograph is Richmonds furniture store, and more than a few young Wolverhampton couples will be able to remember shopping there for a three-piece suite, tables and chairs and a bed for their first home, perhaps paying a little each week on their hire-purchase agreement. Buses have long acted as mobile advertisement hoardings, and the trolley bus in the background advises Wulfrunians to drink Tizer. Without thinking about it we add the words 'The appetizer' - and this is quite understandable considering that the slogan 'Drink Tizer, The Appetizer' was coined back in the 1920s.

Left: High street shopping at its best could be experienced in Dudley Street; this view was captured in April 1975 when the one-way traffic system had been replaced by the pedestrianisation that brought safer shopping to the town's streets.

Leather was very much a fashion statement in the 1970s, and the large poster outside Polly's ladieswear advertises Polly's as 'the skin fashion centre'. Certain groups of people were by that time beginning to swing the tide of public opinion against the wearing of genuine furs, but the early 70s were the heyday of 'fun fur'. Some of our lady readers will no doubt remember with nostalgia their 'ocelot' or 'ermine'; these fake furs might have been cheap but they were not 'tacky'. Stylish and affordable, these fun to wear furs could be seen everywhere. Hepworths Tailoring on the far left was just one of many menswear shops in Wolverhampton - Dunns is on the opposite corner; there were also many shoe shops in the town. Is it just imagination, or are there fewer of them around today? Stylo, Barratts and Turners can all be seen towards the right of the photograph.

Above: This pigeon's eye view gives us a glimpse of Lichfield Street as we rarely see it. How many busy shoppers lift their eyes above the level of a shop window? Yet the tower of St Peter's and the upper windows, rooftops, chimneys and elegant pediments of the building across the road are well worth a few minutes' admiration. Businesses seem to change hands far more often today than they did in earlier years, but these names will still be familiar to many Wulfrunians. On the far left is the premises of Thomas Cook's travel agency; today a famous name throughout the world, Thomas Cook, the Victorian inventor of the package tour, began his modest travel services in Leicester when he planned local train excursions to Loughborough and Derby. The adjoining property is undergoing renovations, while next door to that is James Baker & Sons. Repairwell Ltd were not only cleaners and dyers of clothing but of carpets as well; next along was Necchi, then George Hifkins Ltd, Sketchleys - another dry cleaners - and Boots the chemist. Note the van in the centre of the photograph carrying ladders; it obviously belonged to a firm which was prepared to put its reputation on the line when it advertised its 'Faultless services'.

MANY PROPERTIES ON DARLINGTON STREET WERE DEMOLISHED TO MAKE WAY FOR THE SECOND PHASE OF THE RING ROAD

Above: Trolley buses still ran in Darlington Street at the time this photograph was taken in the 1960s, though their eventual demise was already on the cards. The imposing Clarence House block is in the process of construction in the background. This part of Darlington Street was still a thriving shopping area at the time; mothers could call in at New Joy, on the far left of the photograph, for their baby clothes and equipment; the Wesleyan and General Assurance next door would cater for all their insurance needs, then on the way home they could drop in at the Wimbush Bakers further along for 'naughty but nice' goodies such as doughnuts, iced buns and cream cakes for a teatime treat. There was very little traffic about when this photograph was taken; approaching us from the direction of Lichfield Street is an Austin A40, with a Mini not too far behind. The properties on the left would eventually be demolished as part of the second phase of the Ring Road between Salop Street and Waterloo Road.

Right: Familiar yet unfamiliar; this was Dudley Street in the late 1950s when traffic was still allowed; the concrete lamp standards are typical of the day. Parked at the kerb is a Ford 100E car, with possibly a Rover close behind. Across the road on the corner of Queen Street a row of blinds protect the goods in H Samuel's windows from the sun; the firm survived in the same position for many years. The wording on the corner of the building reminds passers-by that H Samuel were the 'Empire's largest jeweller', a claim that brings to mind the historic days of the British Empire.

H Samuel went in for advertising in a way they probably would not today; note the posters in their upper windows promoting their silver plate and cutlery, their quality Swiss watches and their diamond rings, perfect for an engagement or a gift of distinction. Dudley Street provided banking facilities as well as shopping; in the background readers will perhaps spot the columns around the entrance to Lloyds bank, while the nearby imposing building is Barclays. In the distance the outline of St Peter's Church can be picked out.

Below: An air of desolation hangs over this entire row of properties in Darlington Street. This was 1966; work was about to begin on the second stage of the Ring Road, and days were numbered for this row of once-thriving shops. What were the two people talking about as they chatted on the pavement that day? Were they looking forward to the benefits the Ring Road would bring to the town, or were they perhaps lamenting the passing of an era and the closure of so many small shops? We will never know. All the services and traders that had once served the community had already packed up and departed: the bridal shop where so many brides had chosen their dresses for the big day; the Bingley Building Society, Flint's Opticians, Avion Properties, Glovers' Typewriters, Selwyn, Maitland & Co Estate Agents, the knitting wool shop - all were gone, though not forgotten by the many Wulfrunians who can still ask each other 'Do you remember....' A large number of houses and retail properties were cleared to make way for the enormous Chapel Ash Island that kept traffic flowing smoothly around the town. Work on this phase of the Ring Road was completed by 1968.

Above: The little A35 in the foreground of this evocative photograph of Snow Hill helps us to date it as being from the late 1950s or early 1960s. Many readers will enjoy looking back on their younger days and remembering evenings spent enjoying a pint or three of Atkinsons at the Coach and Horses. Interestingly, the Coach and Horses was advertised 'To Let' when this photograph was taken; the pub is reputed to have a long history as an old coaching inn. Other names in this stretch of roadway will evoke memories: Rudler Brothers opposite the pub, who sold saddles and tack; T J Robinson and Sons, and Coral - not the well-known bookmaker, but a firm of cleaners. A prominent sign outside the tobacconist on the far right advertises Wills Capstan cigarettes. Back then, of course, the campaign against cigarette advertising was beginning to get underway, and in 1965 all cigarette advertising on commercial television was banned. From 1971 advertisers entered into a voluntary agreement with the Department of Health to declare the dangers connected with cigarette smoking, and 'Cigarettes can seriously damage your health' appeared at the foot of adverts, though the word 'seriously' did not appear until 1977.

Right: It was a sad day for Reynolds Restaurant when the popular meeting place finally closed in 1966. The photograph, dated 3rd August of that year, shows a 'To Let' sign in one window, while the blinds were down in the window of Reynolds confectioners. Founded as long ago as 1723, Reynolds established itself through the years as one of the better places to eat. Its beautifully-laid tables with their pristine tablecloths and silver cutlery reinforced its reputation as a very proper establishment where a young lady might meet a man friend without a whiff of scandal. By the 1960s it had become *the* place for ladies to meet for lunch, and the restaurant was sadly missed when it closed down. These buildings remain much the same today, and Reynolds' premises were taken over by the Wolverhampton Tourist Centre. A video shop now occupies the rather pukka premises of Alfred Hall & Son, who were one of the town's more expensive tailors. In the early years of motoring this was the place to go to buy a motoring coat for yourself, or if you were in a position to leave the driving to others, a uniform for your chauffeur.

Bottom: In a scene more reminiscent of the deprived 1930s, three young women (one is almost hidden by the washing) chat one washing day in Court number three, Charles Street, in the 1950s. Few windows survive intact in these courtyard homes, many of which did not even possess running water. Lavatories, shared by two or more families, were outside in the yard; only three of the 101 houses in the Charles Street area had an inside toilet, and only one possessed a bath. The area off Stafford Street was very overcrowded, with a population of 6,335 squashed into 1,639 houses, and these women must have longed with all their souls for somewhere better to bring up their young families. They did not have much longer to wait for their bathrooms, central heating, electric cookers and endless hot water. Designated as a clearance area, Charles Street and Herbert Street were demolished in 1955. Prefabs and new council houses offered a partial solution, followed in the 1960s by a vigorous housing policy that provided high-rise tower blocks at Graisley and The Vauxhalls, with the promise of £1.5m to provide still more blocks in Lower Stafford Street, Blakenhall and Heath Town.

Right: This interesting photograph gives us a fascinating glimpse at the town centre as it might have been. Wallace Wood was the Chief Architectural Assistant and W Mervyn Law was the Borough Engineer and Surveyor when this proposal for a new Wolverhampton Civic Centre was presented. On examination, one of the first questions that springs to

the lips is 'Where is the Town Hall?' One cannot imagine the centre of Wolverhampton without its Victorian elegance; fortunately the Town Hall survived the planners and is still with us, being used today as magistrates' courts. Lichfield Street runs from left to right across the bottom of the proposed centre, with the Royal London building at its junction with Princess Street, Wulfruna Street and Stafford Street, and although we can recognise certain buildings such as The George (now The Varsity) and the parish church, the model has a number of unfamiliar features that obviously never came to fruition. Note the gardens that are attractively laid out where the markets used to be; an example of a proposal that never made it to the finishing post. The new Civic Centre today occupies the open space that once was the ancient market square.

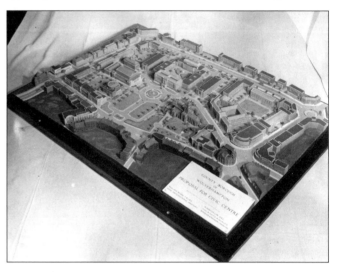

On the move

The date given for this charming view of children at play is June 1955, though the leafless tree in the background would perhaps beg to differ! Was 1955 a particularly cold spring, we wonder. Whatever the temperature, it is not stopping these little boys from having a good time. The little motorist pushing his car into the road will, we presume, today be a big motorist approaching his 50th birthday! Will he - or any of the other boys - recognise themselves and remember that day when some unknown photographer, perhaps a dad or a mum, snapped them as they played?

These boys were playing in Middle Vauxhall; their homes were not too far from Wolverhampton's popular West Park, which presumably they would thoroughly explore and use as a playground as they grew older. The 1950s were still the 'golden' years of childhood, when children were able to roam far and wide in comparative safety, and parents had few of today's worries about allowing them to go beyond the garden gate unaccompanied. Children seem less healthy today when they sit for hours in front of a computer or a TV screen instead of playing out.

Above: The familiar dome of Darlington Street Methodist Church is virtually the only recognisable feature in this photograph of School Street that will stir many memories for readers who knew Wolverhampton as it was. The building on the left that housed the Borough Council Highways Department was destined for demolition along with the adjoining garage, and today a modern block of shops now occupies the place where motorists once filled up with petrol. Beatties' multi-storey car park was to eventually tower above street level on the right of School Street, offering another safe haven for the motorist who ventures into the town centre.

Parked at an unusual angle, a solitary A40 occupies the foreground of this photograph. At first glance the vehicle would appear to present a hazard to traffic until we realise that this section of School Street has been closed to the general public; barriers have been erected across the road in the foreground and background to limit access. As the picture is undated, we can only guess at whether School Street was at this time closed as part of road maintenance, or whether this was the first stage in the demolition and rebuilding work.

Below: Construction work on the Wulfrun Centre is taking place in the background of this photograph of Snow Hill, though the Gaumont Cinema on the far right is still open. There were still five cinemas open in Wolverhampton at the beginning of the 1960s, though there were many more in the 1930s and 40s - the heyday of 'the pictures'. The Gaumont opened in 1932, and it was equipped with dressing rooms and a stage so that it could be used for live performances as well as films. The stage came into its own during the 1960s, when the Gaumont was used for pop concerts, with artists such as Cliff Richard and Gene Vincent performing in front of screaming teenage fans. It closed in November 1973, and Wilkinson's store now occupies the site.

The Central Library can be seen in the background; built to a prizewinning design by Henry Hare the library, which is both stately and elegant, was opened in 1902. This area of the town was well-known for its leisure facilities, and many Wulfrunians will still remember the ABC Cinema, to the left of the library in the photograph, before 1960 when it was still The Savoy.

Below: This section of the Ring Road between the Penn Road roundabout and Salop Street was begun in 1963 and was completed two years later. This photograph was taken in 1965 before the Ring Road continued on to Chapel Ash. An ingenious use was found for this wide central reservation in Peel Street, which provided extra car parking facilities, notably for shoppers using the nearby market. More car parking lies off the photograph to the right. The provision of new car parks was seen as a priority, and a number of multi-storey car parks were built. One of these was Pipers Row, which was built in 1978.

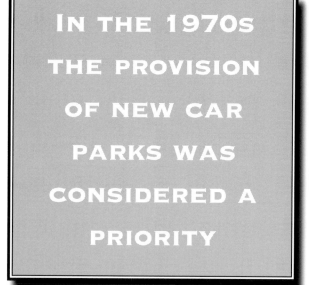

IN THE 1970s THE PROVISION OF NEW CAR PARKS WAS CONSIDERED A PRIORITY

Readers will remember its fate, as less than 20 years later in 1997 it collapsed. Things could have been worse, however - the car park was fortunately empty at the time.

The need for a ring road had been recognised as early as the 1930s, though construction work did not begin until 1960. The Ring Road was laid down in phases; the final section was finished in 1986, 26 years (and many problems) after it was started. The Ring Road has proved to be a major success and is today taken for granted by motorists who forget what a horrendous bottleneck Wolverhampton was for traffic using the A449.

Though the names above the shops may have changed, these Broad Street buildings remain basically the same. The little roundabout being negotiated by these 1960s vehicles, however, was to eventually disappear. Heading up Broad Street past Chick's and Berryman's is a number 11 bus bound for Penn, its side advertising the benefits of shopping at the Co-op.

Of especial interest is the little Mini, still cherished today by the many affectionate owners who managed to hang on to theirs. The Mini was introduced to British drivers in 1959 by Alexander

Issigonis in response to Germany's popular VW Beetle. The Mini's transverse engine made it possible to seat four passengers in comfort in spite of the car only being an incredible ten feet in length. The little vehicle was practical, affordable and fuel-efficient - all features that helped to establish it as a firm favourite, especially with the student population and other hard-up younger drivers. (Perhaps you were one of them!) Issigonis was knighted in 1969 for his contribution to British design, and by the time he died in 1988 more than five million Minis had been sold.

Above: A view of Snow Hill that will be quite unrecognisable to younger readers - the Wulfrun Centre now occupies the place where Allen's Auto Service stood back in 1955, when this photograph was taken. Allen's had quite expansive premises that extended into the adjacent buildings on each side of their main showroom, and were all given the same distinctive mock-Tudor style frontage. They would give you cash for your old car and arrange hire purchase terms to help you buy a new one. Allen's Accessories was more than just an accessories shop selling headlamp bulbs, car mats and different shades of touch-up paint;

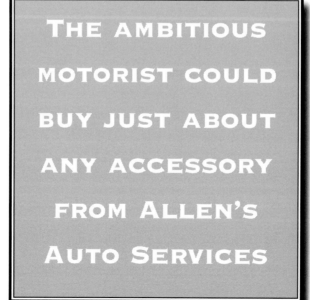

THE AMBITIOUS MOTORIST COULD BUY JUST ABOUT ANY ACCESSORY FROM ALLEN'S AUTO SERVICES

the ambitious motorist could purchase just about anything there including interior lining and roofing materials and carpets. It was the same story with the caravan accessories; Allen's were specialists and could supply materials and equipment from stoves to modern cookers and from aluminium to cans of paint.

Work on the Wulfrun Centre began in 1966 and was carried out in two phases. Today, undercover shopping centres have become a popular and accepted part of modern life, and shoppers running the gauntlet of the British climate can now 'shop till they drop' away from the wind and driving rain.

Below: The official opening of Pendeford Airport in June 1938 was an important occasion, especially as war was once more looming on the horizon. As early as 1937 the Government had realised the potential of air attack in a conflict that even then seemed inevitable. This war would be different from previous wars; planes now had the ability to fly further and carry a heavier load, and the development of new aircraft would be vital to the country. It was Boulton Paul of Pendeford Lane, Fordhouses, who were to make their mark in aircraft construction during the second world war. After the war came a very slow but inevitable decline.

In 1950 huge crowds gathered at Pendeford for the King's Cup Air Race. Among the attractions was Group Captain Peter Townsend who was flying his Hurricane; just five years later he and Princess Margaret were to end their ill-starred romance. The year 1955 also brought the atmosphere of Hollywood to Pendeford, when the airport was the setting for the film 'The Man in the Sky', starring Jack Hawkins.

The airport, however, could not compete with its fast-growing rivals and was eventually closed down. Pendeford was developed to provide sites for much-needed housing, out of town shopping and other services.

Bird's eye view

SAINSBURY'S SAVED ST GEORGE'S CHURCH FROM THE BULLDOZERS WHEN THEY OPENED THEIR NEW STORE IN 1987

Spot the missing Ring Road! The town has moved on since this photograph was taken, and many of these buildings were eventually demolished to make way not only for the new road but for the town's modern shopping centres. Many Wulfrunians will remember St George's church, in the bottom left corner of this photograph, when a thriving congregation met to worship God Sunday by Sunday. The church closed down in 1978, however, and eventually fell into disrepair. This fine building could have been lost for ever, but the Sainsbury's supermarket chain saved it from the bulldozer and incorporated the church into their new store which opened in 1987.

Tracing the line of Lichfield Street, readers will perhaps pick out the imposing frontage of the 73-bedroom Victoria Hotel; back in 1967, bed and breakfast there would have cost you between 41/- and 49/- - that's just over £2 in today's currency. Nearby is the impressive five-storey Chubb's Lock Works in Chubb Street; the building, constructed in 1899, became an exciting and trendy cinema and media centre when Chubbs moved out to premises on the Wednesfield Road. The railway cuts across the top right corner of the photograph, where the High Level Station can be seen.

The heart of the town centre lies beneath us like a three-dimensional map in this aerial view of Wolverhampton. Almost in the centre of the photograph the long rooftops of the Central Arcade can be easily picked out; once a thriving part of the shopping centre its stores closed one by one, and it finally closed down in the late 1960s. Demolition was on the cards for the popular Edwardian arcade despite the campaigning of many Wulfrunians who wanted to preserve it; preservation, however, was not to be, as the Central Arcade was destroyed in a huge fire in May of 1974. Construction of the Mander and the Wulfrun Shopping Centres - both important additions to the town's facilities - has already begun; plans to incorporate a new bus station into the Mander Centre were later dropped. The building to the right of the Central Arcade with the tall chimney is the Manders printing ink works; other well known Wolverhampton landmarks are Beatties department store towards the top right corner, and the Gaumont Cinema in Snow Hill, on the left edge of the photograph. The Gaumont was opened in 1932 and was a popular cinema in its day, but unfortunately succumbed to the countrywide decline in cinema-going and closed its doors in November 1973.

The old Wolverhampton Wanderers stand leads the eye into this aerial view of the town - a sight to bring back many fond memories to supporters who turned out in their thousands over the years to cheer the lads on. The old Molyneux stand, whose wooden gable ends, gold paintwork and wooden seating were familiar to so many was, of course, later replaced by an ultra-modern facility. The Molyneux Hotel and gardens can be seen to the right of the stand - smart and well-used in its heyday, though today facing an uncertain future. The car park at the centre of the photograph once bustled with market traders; today of course the new Civic Centre occupies the site. The old Town Hall to the right is now the Magistrates Court. The prominent group of buildings on the left of the photograph is the Wolverhampton Polytechnic, now the university. In the distance, from the centre to the right, readers with a sharp eye will see that construction work on the first section of the Ring Road between the Dudley Road to the Penn Road Island was actually being carried out when this photograph was taken. This enables us to date the photograph to around 1960, as this first section opened in 1961.

Events & occasions

Above: Taxi firms were fewer in the 1940s and 50s than today, as the ordinary person in the street could rarely afford to pay taxi fares on a regular basis. Certainly they would never think of using a taxi to go shopping or to visit a relative. Most people used public transport or 'shanks' pony' to travel around the town, and for many years taking a taxi was regarded as a luxury that was reserved for events such as weddings, funerals and dire emergencies. Bob's Taxis in Molineux Street was one such established firm, and we can learn from the sign above the window that the proprietor

IN THE 1940S AND 50S MOST PEOPLE USED PUBLIC TRANSPORT OR 'SHANKS PONY' TO GET AROUND

Bob Williams also had a branch office at 55 Clifford Street. Bob offered a versatile day and night service, and, the sign proudly announces, wedding parties were his speciality.

We have no record of who this smartly-dressed group of people were; an educated guess would be that they were one of the many wedding parties that were Bob's principal customers. If so, however, it is not too clear which of these couples is the bride and groom. The best candidates would be the shy-looking young couple on the far right of the picture.

Below: A good day's work well done, and these Birmingham students are relaxing with a cup of tea and taking a well deserved rest at the end of their day's fundraising in Wolverhampton. Their visit was to raise money for local hospitals, and the students dressed up in weird and wonderful costumes and constructed elaborate and eye-catching floats to tempt people out on to the streets to see the procession go by, rattling their collecting boxes under people's noses as they went.

Rag Weeks are still an important part of student life; this particular Rag Week, however, took place a very long time ago, in July 1924 to be exact. This no doubt explains the extreme modesty of the clowns, pirates, Miss Muffets, eastern potentates and cavemen - so different from some of the costumes one might expect Rag Week students to wear 75 years on!

The young people seen enjoying themselves here would have been born soon after the turn of the 20th century, so few of them will be still around today. They chose their path through life, followed a career, married, had families, and made their own contribution to the world. It gives you a moment's sober thought, doesn't it?

Bottom: At long last the long-drawn-out war was over and it was good to be alive, and the residents of Colley Avenue found the energy to let their hair down and organise a party for the local children. Doing the best they could with the ingredients they could get hold of, these mothers managed to conjure up sandwiches, cake, buns and even jelly to give the children a rare treat. Food was strictly rationed - including sweets - and these children had grown up on a basic diet that held few luxuries. Clothing, too, was rationed, and people had to 'make do and mend' whenever they could; by the end of the war most women's wardrobes were looking decidedly tired.

Everyone was looking forward to the future years, to the end of rationing. There was to be no immediate let up in the food rationing that Britain had grown used to during the war, however. In fact a year later in 1946 bread went on ration - though the first bananas that had been seen since before the war arrived from the West Indies. It was 1949 before the nation saw the end of food rationing.

Above: Party hats and broad smiles are in evidence at this huge party held by the residents of Colley Avenue, Low Hill. It was 1945; the war was over, and everybody was tired of gas masks, the blackout, the threat of bombs, and all the other privations of wartime Britain. When peace was declared after six long years of war bunting was strung from house to house across just about every street in Wolverhampton, and patriotic flags flapped gaily in the breeze. Along with the rest of Britain Wulfrunians found the energy to let their hair down and organise Victory Parades, street parties, fireworks displays and bonfires - and this happy scene of children and adults alike enjoying themselves was repeated everywhere across the length and breadth of Great Britain. Unfortunately the names of these children have been lost in the mists of time - apart from one little girl: Mavis Marchant was the girl with pigtails having fun with her friends, on the right. Most of these children will today be senior citizens; what kind of lives did they carve out for themselves? Happy ones, we hope. Perhaps their children and grandchildren are among our readers?

Below: It's party time for every family in Cardiff Street, Penn Fields, and neighbours and friends join together to throw a VE Day party for all the local children. Patriotic flags stir gently in the breeze, and the rousing music from the barrel organ on the left lends its own lively contribution to the occasion. World War II had been a difficult time for mothers with families to feed, and though everyone had enough to eat there were few luxuries around. Food, clothing and other goods were strictly rationed and the newspapers published recipes for plain dishes such as oatmeal sausages, beetroot soup, eggless cake and carrot jam. 'Woman's Hour' presenters gave hints and tips on how to make a little go a long way. Children born during the war had never seen a banana before, and they had no idea that they had to peel off the skin before they could eat them. For a good while to come saccharin tablets still went into tea cups in place of sugar, and whale oil margarine was still spread on the nation's bread. Several years were to pass before people could stop using tinned dried eggs, or shop for clothes without counting how many coupons they had.

Below: Harrowby Road, Bilston was the scene of this marvellous knees-up staged in June 1953 to celebrate the Queen's coronation. Bunting flapped gaily from many windows, and the kiddies are ready to wave their union jacks. Some, like the joker in drag in the far left foreground, have donned fancy dress for the occasion; others, like the man on the right in the natty waistcoat, did not need it.

The day was cool and it was inclined to drizzle, but that certainly did not stop Harrowby Road from having a good time!

Perhaps a few people among the crowd would have been able to watch the crowning of the Queen in Westminster Abbey on television; it was the first time the coronation of a British monarch had ever been filmed.

Television sets were expensive, however, and though Britain had a television service as early as 1936, few people could afford to buy them - and the range of programmes was very limited anyway. By the 1950s sets were beginning to get cheaper, and the Queen's Coronation presented many families with the ideal reason to buy or rent a TV set. Those who didn't simply crowded into the parlours of more fortunate neighbours to watch the event!

THE QUEEN'S CORONATION IN 1953 PROVIDED MANY FAMILIES WITH THE IDEAL REASON TO BUY A TV SET

Was Oxford Street in Bilston really a one-way street back in 1953 - or has this motorist driving on the right been celebrating the Queen's coronation a little too freely? The White Rose, along with every other pub in the town, probably fared quite well on 2nd June 1953.

The coronation gave everyone a chance to declare their loyalty to the Queen - and we can see from this photograph that it was party time in Swan Bank. Union Jacks and garlands were hung from every available window, lines of bunting stretched across every street,

and though the weather on the big day was inclined to be cool and rather damp, it didn't stop the people of Bilston from enjoying themselves.

When the Queen was crowned in a Westminster Abbey service on 2nd June 1953, A mere eight years after the end of World War Two, the nation relaxed for the first time and really went to town on the celebrations that welcomed the Queen to the throne. Each town and city, every village institute and church, held their own event, which could range from a simple street party to a big parade.

Above: Bilston Carnival was a popular and regular event in the town, and large crowds would gather to greet the Carnival Queen as she rode past enthroned on her beautifully-decorated float, complete with elegant marble columns reminiscent of ancient Greece. This was the 1956 Carnival Queen, and she and her attendants are wearing smiles of genuine enjoyment as they wave to the waiting crowds. The richly gowned young lady sitting at the front of the float is likely to have been the retiring Carnival Queen. The attendants include several little girls, for whom the carnival would have been a red-letter day. How they would have enjoyed dressing up for the occasion in their pretty dresses! Somebody had obviously been very busy for weeks, perhaps months, beforehand, producing all the necessary 'props', and measuring, cutting and sewing all these marvellous costumes.

Note the collecting box that one of the young ladies is holding; no doubt a large part of their responsibility that day was to do a lot of box-rattling as they passed among the good-natured Wulfrunians enjoying the carnival atmosphere, expecting them to dig deep in their pockets and support the charitable cause.

Shopping spree

Below: The 1930s were part of a gentler age that existed without the frenetic charge of polluting traffic along the Ring Road. Those were the days when you could safely leave your pram outside the doorway for a couple of minutes while you popped into George Mason's to buy a quarter of tea or a pound of bacon. And you could park your bicycle at the kerb and expect to find it still there when you returned from your shopping expedition; how long would this cycle standing outside Marks & Spencer's stay put today, we wonder? This photograph was obviously taken at the time dreaded by every schoolboy, those days towards the end of the summer holidays when mothers hauled them off to try on new shirts and stiff new school jackets and trousers. Marks & Spencer - who still occupy the same space - were advertising their 'Back to School' boys' wear department. Their fathers could have shopped at Southan Bros gents outfitters, further down Dudley Street. The lovely old saloon car parked at the kerb in the foreground would have belonged to one of Wolverhampton's rather more affluent citizens; few working people could afford the luxury of a family car back in the 1930s.

The new retail market in 1961, a year after it was opened by Lord Morrison of Lambeth. The Wolverhampton Chronicle termed the new markets as a half a million pound gamble; the modern facility had cost around £508,000, yet the conservative punters of Wolverhampton were by no means bound to enjoy shopping in a market that had been described as too 'European' for the town. Over the three years it took to build the markets, officials were still arguing about one or other aspect of the project. Eventually, of course, it came to be accepted as part of Wolverhampton's shopping area. The outdoor stalls with their brightly-striped awnings fell short of modern standards, however, and seven years later permanent concrete stalls were constructed.

The right to hold a market in Wolverhampton dates back nearly 750 years - though back in 1180 some enterprising traders conveniently 'forgot' that they needed a licence, only to get fined for their cheek.

It had been hoped that the site of the open market would be kept as open space, but after it had been used for car parking for some time, the Civic Centre was eventually constructed and opened in the late 1970s.

Above: A trip down memory lane for readers who remember Dudley Street in the days before the many sweeping changes brought the Mander Centre to Wolverhampton. Singleton & Cole Ltd were the tobacconists on the right, while on the far left of the photograph is the Kings Head pub which was built around the turn of the 20th Century. The building at the centre of this 1930s photograph was home to two outfitters; who remembers shopping at W Evans and Melias? Back then housewives did their shopping at the small grocery chains such as Melias, where customers would queue to be served while the assistant weighed out butter from a huge slab and sliced bacon while you waited - a far cry from today's plastic packs! People might have to wait a while longer to be served, but at least they had the benefit of personal attention from the staff.

Further to the left is the ill-starred Central Arcade. The decision to demolish this well-loved landmark was fought tooth and nail by protesters who wanted it to be integrated into the design of the new shopping centre, but in the end it was fire that signalled the arcade's final demise.

Above right: Do you remember visiting the Co-op Family Fare Exhibition? It is interesting to speculate on what the exhibits were - and why the event was staged. Note, too, that admission to the exhibition was free; a contrast to the present day when few events of any description can boast free admission! The size of this canvas exhibition hall suggests that the show was a very ambitious event. Sharp-eyed readers might pick out the 'E II R' logo that was so common during Coronation year, which together with the (probably) red, white and blue garlands that festoon the frontage, would pinpoint the year to 1953.

The Co-operative movement started more than a century ago in Rochdale, where a group of 28 local people paid £1 each to buy goods and open a shop. Customers were awarded a dividend on everything they bought. The idea caught on in a big way, and eventually there were enough societies to have their own suppliers, and beginning with footwear, soap and biscuits the CWS began to manufacture its own goods. During the earlier years of the 20th Century the Co-op movement was responsible for a vast improvement in the standard of living of the average British working class person.

The foreman rings his bell to signal the end of another market day; perhaps the ladies around the stall on the far right had lingered until the end to take advantage of any last minute bargains. You could usually expect to pay a few coppers less for fruit and vegetables in the market than in the high street shops, and at closing time there were often real bargains to be snapped up if you happened to be in the right place at the right time.

This photograph dates back to 1952, and the clothes worn by some of these shoppers still reflect the wartime styles of the previous decade; after all, clothing was rationed up until 1949. During the 1950s older ladies almost without exception favoured a neat little hat, while the younger women still opted to wear the very practical headscarf, that could be folded away in a pocket or handbag, and brought out in wind or rain. These ladies were in good company - Her Majesty has long been a keen wearer of headscarves.

The rather nice wholesale market building forms the backdrop to this picture. A new wholesale market at Stow Heath eventually replaced it; functional - but visually not a patch on the 1902 version!

Left: A good way, perhaps, to earn a little extra pocket money? It was 1952, and a few bob extra to spend on sweets and comics or perhaps a visit to the cinema would have been very welcome to these young boys helping out in the market. The boy wearing his school cap is concentrating fiercely on untying the knot on the string that is securing a crate of Spanish onions - though we can't see what the other youngster behind the pile of boxes is doing. In the shadow of the old wholesale market, a number of shoppers at the stall behind them pause to browse and to pick out a selection of the best fruit and vegetables - and the subject uppermost in their minds is likely to be concerned with deciding whether to spec out and buy a cauliflower, or to stick with cabbage (cheaper, though perhaps less popular with the children!) to go with their Sunday roast this week.

Above: A nostalgic view of the market place taken from the well-manicured gardens of St Peter's church, first

THE WELL MANICURED GARDENS OF ST PETER'S CHURCH WERE FIRST LAID OUT OVER 100 YEARS AGO

laid out more than a hundred years ago. The church itself, which dates from 1425, has changed little since the 16th century, apart from the chancel which underwent extensive reconstruction work in 1867. Many Wulfrunians have made the long but immensely rewarding trek to the top of the church tower at least once in their lives, taking advantage of the opening up to visitors once a year of the tower steps - more than 900 of them. Those who have braved the long haul, counting, no doubt, as they go, assure the less agile among us that the wonderful view of the woods, the town and the far countryside, is well worth the aching leg muscles. Pity the poor soul who loses count halfway up and has to start all over again! The wholesale fruit and vegetable market stands on the right of the photograph; while it stood, how many shoppers ever stopped to admire the building's ornate brickwork and its little towers and domes? Sadly it disappeared in 1973, 70 years after it first opened.

Tulips, daffodils, irises, narcissi - all were there on that spring day in 1960, and these girls who have already treated themselves to a choc ice (or are they bars of chocolate?) are debating whether to treat themselves - or, one likes to think, their mothers - to a bunch of cheerful flowers. The fashions are typical of the late 50s and early 60s, though for practicality's sake the flower seller is still wearing the 'turban' that was popular during the 1940s. Note the open baskets used by these young women; thirty years ago people need not be quite as aware of thieves and pickpockets as we unfortunately have to be today.

This was the open market's last day before it moved lock, stock and barrel to its new School Street site along with the covered market.

The Roman Catholic church of Ss Peter and Paul in North Street can be seen in the background on the left; plans to demolish the church and the adjoining Giffard House were scotched in the 1980s following a vigorous campaign to keep the historic building. Nearby is the wholesale market which was demolished during the 1970s to make way for the Civic Centre.

Below: The name 'Temple of Fashion' was cut into the stone atop Willsons upmarket ladieswear store in Dudley Street. The shop opened with a flourish in the 1920s as costumiers and furriers, and a surprising number of men were present at its grand opening. A decade or so later the shop was in need of refurbishment, and the facade and windows pictured here were the end result of the renovations. There was a grand gala opening in 1937, and this photograph was taken after dark to show the illuminated signs at their very best.

the arcaded windows were decorated in style with a wide selection of costumes, coats, skirts, blouses, hats and jackets. Closer inspection of the mannequins tells us that big collars were in vogue

at the time. A beautiful evening gown of silk or satin is displayed in the window at the rear of the arcade. The reopening presented the ladies of the town with an opportunity to acquire a free hat; notices in the windows advise passers-by that a smart hat would be presented free with every outfit purchased. An offer that could not be refused. In time the store that was so popular in its heyday closed down, and Marks and Spencer took over the site.

Bottom: It was obviously a cold day when this brisk market day scene was caught on camera 45 years ago in 1954; awnings were up to protect the goods and the traders from rain and wind, and the punters had all donned woolly hats and heavy coats for their shopping trip. The row of cars parked below the wall of St Peter's church give us a pleasant trip back in time and present an interesting contrast between the somewhat austere lines of the Ford Popular, typical of earlier decades, and the lighter, more rounded lines of post-war cars like the A35 van and the Austin car on the right, when colour was introduced into motor car design. In its day the Ford Popular was a very affordable little vehicle, and more than one among our readers will no doubt remember the 'Ford Pop' with fondness as their very first car. Do you remember the strange layout of the gears, with reverse where first gear would be on other cars? And the hand-brake placed below the dashboard? And the vacuum wipers that gave up when you put your foot down and flogged away like mad when you eased off the accelerator? All part of this great little vehicle's character.

Above: Another busy day in the old open air market back in 1959, and you can almost recapture that familiar 'market day' atmosphere. It was a dry day, so few canvas awnings have been put in place over the stalls, though the hats and coats worn by all the shoppers would indicate that the weather was not too warm. The Saturday market was much looked forward to by many wives who during the week were tied to the house and the children; has the new open market generated the same kind of affection among the shoppers of today?

The indoor market can just be seen on the far left of the photograph, and Giffard House on the right. Interestingly, a mass X-ray unit was in Wolverhampton at the time, and people were being encouraged to attend - note the banner in the right background. This was almost certainly one of the mass chest X-ray facilities that was set up to deal 'once and for all' with tuberculosis, and these mobile units did a very good job in diagnosing any problems. The development of antibiotics offered some hope that the disease (which was at one time the leading cause of death in the Western world) would be eradicated - but it was not to be.

Above right: Readers will notice that most of these browsing shoppers are women. We have no exact date for the photograph, but the style of dress would indicate the 1950s; 50 years or so ago far more men went out to work while their wives cared for the home and family and made sure there was a hot meal waiting on the table at the end of the day. The 1950s were years of progress when families could afford washing machines and vacuum cleaners, and the spin-off from that was that

housework took less time, freeing women to find a job that would give them the extra cash they needed. The total lack of traffic travelling along Dudley Street is worth drawing attention to; two women have chosen the roadway to get together for a cosy chat, while a lone man walks heedlessly in the middle of the road. Traffic was to become a hazard to shoppers in the town centre, and Dudley Street and this section of Queen Street would later become pedestrian shopping areas - far safer for parents with buggies to cope with and small children to keep an eye on.

The properties with the curious pointed gables have now gone, of course, and Lloyds Bank, whose side wall we can detect in the background, was later extended.

This patriotic market trader has taken advantage of the open market's final day to create an imaginative and eye-catching display that perhaps attracted a number of extra customers. The Union Jacks and the royal banners displaying the crown and that famous portrait of Her Majesty have perhaps been packed away in a cupboard since the coronation seven years earlier, but now they have been taken out to mark another, rather sadder, occasion. The stars and stripes of the USA share a colourful spot in front of the stall, though the sign that perhaps tells us why these particular flags are there is unfortunately obscured by a customer buying fruit and vegetables. This trader offers a good choice of fresh produce; he has something to suit most tastes: extra large oranges were only 3d each while best bananas were just 1/2d a pound - that's around six new pence in today's currency, if not in value; he has some fine-looking cauliflowers, and the potatoes, a notice tells us, 'eat like Jerseys' at 6d a pound. Note, though, the lack of vegetables such as peppers, broccoli and sweet potatoes that we take for granted today.

Below: Will it go with the dark blue carpet and curtains - or won't it? And shall we have the embossed paper or the smooth? This lady choosing new wallpaper has settled down in comfort to do the job properly, making it clear that no decision is imminent. The bored youngster (is this her son?) has obviously given up all hopes of making a quick getaway, and we have to wonder what is going through his mind as he sits gazing absently into space nibbling on a bread bun. Meanwhile, perhaps Mum should be keeping an eye on her unattended shopping bag, though people were perhaps more honest in the 1950s. Saturday has traditionally been the most favoured shopping day, and people who during the week were at work in the office or the factory looked forward to the weekly trip to the town centre shops and markets. At the time this photograph was taken the old Victorian covered market in Cheapside was just over 100 years old. And weren't those Victorians inventive? They made the slender iron pillars that supported the roof hollow so that they could be used to carry away rainwater directly into the drains. Very ingenious.

Above: It was springtime when this typical market scene was caught by the photographer. Springtime; symbolic of new life and fresh beginnings - yet ironically this spring day in 1960 signalled the end of the town's open retail market. It was the last time the women in this photograph would buy flowers from this particular flower stall, and shoppers and market traders alike would no doubt have already been feeling the usual sense of loss when an old and familiar part of life is replaced by something new and untried.

It was with the market's move from its old position in St Peter's Square to its new site in School Street on Brick Kiln Patch that the symbolism of new beginnings would apply. The new beginnings affected not just the market but the entire town, and the closing of the open market was only the first of the many changes that were to hit Wolverhampton in the following years.

Right: This little chap appears to be heartily sick of shopping -

a feeling typical of most children who are dragged unwillingly around the shops by their busy mums. The traders in the background appear to be packing up at the end of the day, so the little boy could not have had too much longer to wait. Note his mother's brown carrier bag with string handles. They don't make them like that any more! Weren't paper carriers more friendly to the environment than today's ubiquitous plastic carrier that blows around in the wind, gets stuck in trees and hedges and generally makes an eyesore of both town and country?

The union jack hanging from one of the stalls reminds us that this was the last day of trading for the market; both the indoor and open markets were soon to move to their new site. In recent years came yet more changes; work began in 1996 on the open market's newest site in pedestrianised School Street. All part of the town's plans for further redevelopment between School Street and Snow Hill.

At work

Major redevelopments at the junction of Salop Street and School Street gave pedestrians a good excuse for indulging in what, it might be suspected, is one of Britain's favourite hobbies - staring into holes that have been dug in the road.

The new subway that was to give shoppers direct access from the main shopping area to the markets was under construction, and there was plenty of activity going on here to keep the most curious passer-by happy: a crane aiding the construction workers with the heavy lifting, workmen digging, men sorting timber and shoring up the sides of the

trench, foremen checking the progress of the work - and all without a hard hat in sight. It is interesting to note that the ubiquitous flat cap is the preferred workwear in this photograph. 'No hat, no boots, no job' is the slogan that reflects today's strict emphasis on workers' safety, but even comparatively recently workmen undertook many dangerous jobs every day without gauntlets, safety glasses, hard hats or protective clothing of any kind, and reflected very little on the risk factor. In fact, in some occupations it was regarded as being somewhat less than macho to wear protective clothing!

The long-established company whose products make newspaper headlines every day

The centre of Wolverhampton has been home to Mander family businesses for more than two and a quarter centuries. In the second half of the 18th century Benjamin Mander ran a japan and tinplate business - japanning meant decorating items such as trays, firescreens, wine-coolers, clocks and ornamental cupboards, and required a high degree of skill and artistry - and his next door neighbour and brother, John, had a chemical works.

Benjamin had a son called Charles who clearly took a lively interest in his father's work; he began to conduct his own experiments with varnish over the kitchen fire, proving, amongst other things, that varnish should not be put into the cooking pots. A series of culinary disasters occurred, and Charles and his equipment were banished to the garden shed.

The raw ingredients of the first varnishes were rosin, oil and turpentine, to which were added some liquid driers. When Charles took the business over after his father's death in 1819 he regarded varnishes as a product to be sold as well as to be used, and gradually the manufacture and sale of varnish took over from japan to become the main focus of the business. The firm was appointed to supply varnish to George III, and in 1845 two of Charles' sons, Charles B and Samuel S Mander, went into partnership to form Mander Brothers. Their business prospered. By 1865 the Colour Works had been set up, and colour and paint proved a very profitable business. The company opened an office in London and set up a number of overseas depots or agencies in countries such as France, Italy, Canada and Australia. Meanwhile the Mander family fortunes grew, and over the years the family rose to a position of eminence, playing a part in local government, holding such offices as Mayor of Wolverhampton and Member of Parliament, performing philanthropic acts such as the institution of University scholarships and in several cases being accorded honours by the monarch of the

Above: Benjamin Mander, one of the founders of the Manders' family businesses. Below: Specialist painting at Townwell Works in the late 1920s.

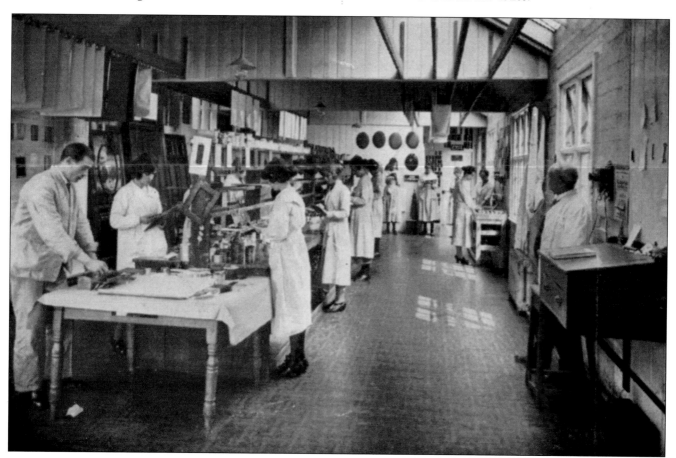

day. Amongst the fine family residences was Wightwick Manor, built by Samuel Theodore Mander in 1887 and given to the National Trust in 1937.

Mander Brothers Limited came into existence in the 1920s, when the management of the firm was in the hands of only surviving grandson of Charles Mander, Sir Charles Tertius Mander Bart., and the next generation of sons - Charles Arthur, Gerald, Geoffrey and Howard Vivian Mander. The paint and printing ink works were moved from the centre of Wolverhampton to the firm's existing site approximately one mile outside the town, while the varnish plant and head office remained in the town centre. The next 30 years were a time both of organic growth and of acquisition, from which the company emerged as one of the the largest printing ink manufacturers in the UK, trading as Mander-Kidd, as well as an established decorative paint and wallpaper merchant. In 1937 a public company was formed and quoted on the London Stock Exchange. During the 60s a completely new venture was launched; after much careful planning and major investment, the site of the original house and works was developed into a five-acre shopping centre, the ever-popular Mander Centre of today. The freehold of this retail complex served to enhance the assets of the Group, and the establishment of the Property Division provided a secure base for the Group's progressive trading activities.

In 1972 the active involvement of the Mander family in the business came to an end after some 200 years with the death of Philip Fitzgerald Mander, then Chairman of the public company.

The 1980s saw Manders established amongst the leaders in the development and production of high quality decorative paints, printing inks and industrial finishes; also, by acquiring competitive businesses whose activities complemented its own, and integrating their products into the Group, it had become a major distributor of decorative products including tiles and wallcoverings; and, of course, it was the proprietor of a major shopping centre in Wolverhampton. However, the keenly competitive climate in the paint and printing ink industry, highlighted by an unsuccessful takeover bid from a competitor in 1992, spurred Manders to review its long-term strategy. As a result, it was decided to focus on the higher technology activities of printing inks with the ability to serve its growing number of customers internationally. From the end of 1993 and throughout 1994, Manders embarked on a transformation which involved the sale of its decorative paint business and the Mander Centre and the acquisition of a number of ink businesses worldwide. This programme of acquisitions included the ink businesses of Croda, a major competitor with paste, liquid inks and graphic supplies operations in the UK, Ireland, Italy, the Netherlands, New Zealand and Zimbabwe and subsequently its inks operation in the USA. In the middle of 1994, Premier Inks based in the Netherlands and one of Europe.s

Above: Heath Town Works in the 1950s.

leading manufacturers of publication inks, was acquired and, later in the year, Morrison Inks of New Zealand. This gave Manders a strong presence in Europe, Australasia and the USA. In 1996 Manders completed its acquisitions with a large facility in Sweden specialising in metal decorating coatings. Its various European locations have now been developed into six centres of excellence specialising in news inks, publication inks, commercial sheetfed inks, liquid inks for packaging and metal decorating inks. In 1997 some 60 countries were supplied through 28 manufacturing and distribution centres throughout the world and printing ink sales had increased from £40million in 1993 to £160million in 1997. Overall, some 60 countries are supplied through 28 manufacturing and distribution centres throughout the world.

Here in Wolverhampton, the Mander factory has become the company's Centre of Excellence for the manufacture of coldset inks which are used in newspapers. Newspaper inks dry by absorption onto the paper as it is being printed, and today's technology means that printing presses not only run at much higher speeds, printing over 20 papers every second, but also print in colour, which is produced from a mixture of black, yellow, blue and red. The properties of the inks must therefore allow them to superimposed on top of each other at these speeds and dry as they are being printed. The company invests heavily in research and development, with a team of highly-qualified chemists constantly evaluating raw materials for improved performance, to keep pace with the constant technical demands of the markets and to ensure that customers' needs are being met. The high-quality inks produced

*Above: Some recent samples of the company's product in use. **Top right:** A paint mixing machine. **Right:** Part of the modern transport fleet.*

at Wolverhampton are supplied to most of the national daily newspapers and a significant number of provincial newspapers, including the Express & Star printed in Wolverhampton, West Bromwich and Telford. Because Manders has a particular expertise in the reproduction of colour, the company was the manufacturer chosen by Eddie Shah when he launched the "Today" newspaper, the first UK daily to use colour. The number of overseas customers has also grown in recent years, and now includes newspapers in Germany, the Netherlands, France and Scandinavia. The company's future plans include continuing investment in new technology at Wolverhampton to consolidate its position as one of the most efficient producers of newspaper inks, and also to provide the capacity to develop the overall European market share.

In 1998 Manders was acquired by the Flint Ink Corporation of America, which combines all the advantages of being the largest privately-owned ink manufacturer in the world with those of being a family-owned company. High values and principles and a commitment to quality are just some of the legacies which the illustrious Mander family has given to Wolverhampton over the centuries, and those values are still alive in the company today.

The key to success!

Rising crime statistics and new initiatives in crime prevention may sound to us like a typical 20th-century headline, but keeping out unwanted visitors is by no means a new problem. Not long after the battle of Waterloo the British public was already complaining about the increase in crime, and specifically theft of property. The earliest version of the security lock has been in use since the 1770s, but it was in 1818 that Charles and Jeremiah Chubb patented their Detector Lock, and the underlying principle of the Detector Lock is still at the basis of lock construction today.

Both Chubb brothers had served their apprenticeships to a blacksmith in Winchester. In 1804 Charles moved to Portsea, Portsmouth, where he opened a

shop specialising in naval ironmongery, supplying and repairing the tremendous variety of metal parts which were required by the sailing ships of the day. Following the brothers' invention of the Detector Lock, however, Charles tranferred his attention to the manufacture and sale of locks, and the brothers set up a factory in Temple Street, Wolverhampton; Wolverhampton was chosen because of its long-standing reputation as home to the very best locksmiths. The Chubb lock rapidly came to be regarded as the best of its kind; in 1923 George IV

granted the first Chubb Special Licence - Special Licences being the forerunner of Royal Warrants - and since then Chubb locks have consistently enjoyed Royal favour, making Chubb one of the oldest continuous Royal Warrant holders in the country. Chubb's customers in 1828 included the Duke of Wellington who bought four locks and a new key for Aspley House, and the Bank of England who bought two locks at six guineas each. At least one rival Wolverhampton locksmith resented the Chubbs' success: Thomas Hart, one such well-known locksmith, boasted that he could pick Chubb's lock and advertised a time at which he proposed to do so in public; but he did not turn up. A reward of £10 was offered, and this time he took up the challenge, but failed to open the lock, even though, having failed to pick it, he resorted to trying to make a key to fit - which many people considered to be cheating. Other locksmiths tried, and also failed, and in the end their attempts served only to establish beyond any doubt the superiority of the Chubb lock.

Chubb's first patent for a burglar-resisting safe was taken out in 1835, although it is thought that safes were being made by the firm before this date. From the mid 1830s on, the manufacture of safes, vaults and safe deposits became as important a part of the firm's activity as was the manufacture of locks; a factory was set up in Cowcross Street, London, in 1837 to make safes and strongroom doors, while the Wolverhampton factory concentrated on lock manufacture.

By the time of Charles Chubb's death in 1846 'Chubb' had become a household word, to such an extent that it was appearing on playbills and in popular verses of the time. The business was carried on after Charles' death by his son and partner, John Chubb.

The Great Exhibition of 1851 sparked off keen Anglo-American competition when an American locksmith named Hobbs succeeded in picking one of Chubb's locks, although it was generally agreed that the conditions under which he worked were quite unlike any that a burglar would ever encounter. For a while the Great Lock Controversy raged; and British pride and honour were finally vindicated when one of Chubb's employees worked out how to pick Hobbs' lock, and gave a successful public demonstration. One positive outcome of this controversy was Chubb's introduction of a small and brilliantly simple modification, the barrel and

Left: Early deliveries of Chubb's safes.

curtain, which prevents two picks from being inserted into the lock, thereby making it unpickable, as it is not possible to open the mechanism using a single pick.

John Chubb died in 1872 and was succeeded by his sons John Charles, George Hayter and Harry Withers. By this time the London safe factory had moved from Cowcross Street to premises in Glengall Road, off the Old Kent Road, which gave accommodation about equal in area to the Wolverhampton works. In 1882 the lease on the Wolverhampton factory expired. It was decided that a new factory should be built to mark the firm's centenary, and so the lock works temporarily moved to London while

the new Wolverhampton factory was under construction. During this period the firm started to branch out in several directions; it began to manufacture ecclesiastical ornaments, art metalwork and decorative ironwork including bolts, and it also expanded into the export market, opening a depot in Cape Town, South Africa and setting up a distribution company in Sydney, Australia. It also introduced another important innovation, which it was prompted to developed in response to the crime wave from which America suffered during the 1870s; this was the Time Lock, a clockwork or electrically-operated mechanism which prevents a safe door from opening before a pre-set length of time has elapsed.

In 1899 the new Wolverhampton factory, which comprised both a lock works and a safe-making department, each capable of accommodating 350 workmen, was opened amid great celebrations. For the next ten years both the London and the Wolverhampton factories continued to operate, but in 1908 the Glengall Road factory was closed and all its operations, together with the London workforce, were transferred to Wolverhampton, where another new works had been built. Over the years, as the workforce had grown and as the management had been handed down from one generation of the Chubb family to the next, a strong sense of staff loyalty had built up, with annual picnics and outings attended by management and workers becoming established customs.

The firm continued to look after its employees during the first world war, when, for all the men who enlisted, it made up the difference between their army pay and the amount they would have earned in the factory. The outbreak of war brought orders for a wide range of military equipment: safes for the Admiralty and the Army, armour plating for cars and subsequently tanks, bulkhead doors for ships, mine sinkers, tank peephole cover apparatus, and of course immense numbers of high explosive and shrapnel shells; during 1918, up to 4,000 shells a week were produced by a workforce consisting largely of women and young people under military age.

Below: The company premises in the early 1930s.

The Chairman at this time was George Hayter Chubb. His distinguished career had already earned him a knighthood, and in 1928 he was created a Baron. Ten years later multiple celebrations took place, marking the 120th anniversary of the company, Lord Hayter's 90th birthday and retirement as Chairman (although he remained a managing director until his death eight years later), and the opening of an extension to the Wolverhampton works which brought the total factory area to over six and a half acres.

The second world war again created its own special demands, and this time the company was called upon to make turrets for tanks, armoured bodies for scout cars, mounts for guns, smoke mortars, ramps for landing craft, and locks and gauges of all varieties.

Following Lord Hayter's death in 1936, his nephew Harry Emory Chubb became Chairman. Expansion and modernisation continued; in 1947 the decision was made to introduce mechanised production, which enabled the company to market a range of machine-made locks offering a high degree of security at a very reasonable price. A selection of hand-made locks for specialised functions was retained; and one of the commissions which the company undertook the following year was very specialised indeed - improvements and additions to the security of the Crown Jewels in the Tower of

London. Four years later the company also became responsible for the security of the Persian Crown Jewels and the Peacock Throne when it won the contract for the security installation at Bank Melli, Iran. In that year, too, Chubb became one of the few companies to exhibit in both the 1851 and 1951 Festivals of Britain, when it showed a trend-setting vault door which was subsequently installed for a leading Canadian insurance company. Three years later a Canadian subsidiary company was formed, and manufacturing began in Canada.

Continual development of security products has always been necessary to keep ahead of new methods of attack. In the mid-1900s oxygen-cutting became increasingly used as a method of safe-breaking; up to 1954 only banking houses and specialised organisations had invested in this kind of protection because of the prohibitive cost, but Chubb then made a technical breakthrough which allowed them to introduced a new range of reasonably-priced safes, the Chubb Standard Anti-Slowpipe Safe, to combat this method of attack. In 1959 the company introduced a special alloy known as Anti-Arc material which increased protection against oxy-arc cutting, and in 1962 safes became safer still with the development of another new alloy known as TDR, or Torch and Drill Resisting.

Above: Today's modern service fleet.

Meanwhile, H Emory Chubb had done much to increase Chubb's export activities, and his successor, the Honourable G C H Chubb, continued this work. The Lock and Safe Company of Rhodesia (Pvt) Limited was formed; the Canadian subsidiary merged to form Chubb-Mosler and Taylor Safes Limited; and the Chubb Lock and Safe Company was formed in New Zealand to manufacture and market security products. The company also expanded into a broader range of security products, mainly through acquisition; the International Coin Counting Machine Company which specialises in all kinds of coin changing and dispensing machines joined the Chubb Group in 1961; Burgot Alarms Limited added alarm systems to Chubb's range of equipment, Read and Campbell Limited brought fire extinguishing equipment under the Chubb umbrella, and the Pyrene Company Limited brought further diversification in 1967 with its range of fire protection systems and detection equipment, products for the motor vehicle industry and specialised metal finishing processes. Also in 1967, Chubb acquired Fraigneux, Belgium's oldest safe manufacturer, and formed NV Chubb Fraigneux SA, thus putting itself in a position to operate effectively in the EC. In 1968 the firm moved into the cash dispenser market, with its first cash dispenser unit at the Victoria Street branch of the Westminster Bank; so that by the end of its first 150 years in business, Chubb had built upon its expertise and reputation in lock and safe manufacture to expand into a number of related areas, and established itself as a market leader across the world.

In the past two decades, huge investment in research and development has ensured that the company's security products have kept many steps ahead of potential attackers and several steps ahead of the competition; and also that the range of products offered continues to meet the increasingly sophisticated needs of technological progress. Using a combination of the finest design concepts, expert engineering, the best materials and the latest manufacturing technology, Chubb products offer the most effective fire and burglar resistant equipment available today, ensuring the safety and security of valuable items and vital information, be it in paper or electronic format. Modern safes, for instance, need to resist all known methods of unauthorised access for as long as possible, even if attack methods and tools are used in combination; so, firstly, Chubb provides a strong anchorage facility in the base of the safe to prevent bodily removal to a discreet place for uninhibited attack. Then, high quality locks, incorporating devices such as 'false notches'

and curtain levers, frustrate lock-picking attempts, with hard inclusions in the barrier material to counter attempts at drilling or optical fibre viewing. The properties of the alloys developed for barrier material make it resistant to penetration from oxy-arc cutting equipment and diamond drills, and the elimination of corner joints through monolithic construction makes delamination extremely difficult. Additional features to assure the protection of electronic media include fire resisting barrier material, and even a reinforced plinth which provides maximum energy absorption to protect the contents if the floor of a building collapses when on fire. Finally, all Chubb products undergo the most stringent testing to the strictest international standards, to ensure that each product more than fits the purpose for which it was designed. For example, as part of the VDMA S120P test a red hot cabinet is dropped 9.1 metres onto rubble, and then reheated, to ensure that it will still provide protection in the event of floor collapse.

Chubb offers a range of quality security products to suit all customers, from the largest world banking organisation to the individual with cash or valuables to protect. Additionally, technical experts are available to give advice from six strategically-placed service depots covering the UK, and from Chubb's own depots or its network of exclusive distribution outlets overseas. Europe, Africa, the Americas and the Middle East continue to be the company's main export markets, with a growing trade in Scandinavia and Eastern Europe.

With more than 180 years' experience in making security products, Chubb's aims remain the same: to maintain its worldwide reputation as the manufacturer of the best security products available.

Below: A current day Chubb Safe.

'Praise God and pass the ammunition!'

The Royal Ordnance factory at Featherstone has played a vital part in the nation's defence since it was set up in the desperate days of 1940/41. Originally built in 1940, on a site partly occupied by Courtaulds the Coventry textiles manufacturer, to fill artillery shells provided by other works, the exigencies of war brought rapid changes.

The early years of the mobile desert war of the North African campaigns quickly brought to light the superiority of the now ubiquitous 'Jerry-can' as an all-purpose liquid container which did not fall apart under active service conditions, and of the enemy's armour-piercing shells which had such devastating effect not only on the early lightweight tanks such as the Matilda but on later heavier models too. Fortunately British forces captured great stocks of these items which were sent home for appraisal and reproduction and ultimate effective use against a well-prepared enemy.

Below: Wartime buildings and railway lines. The Carbide Recovery section in the 1960s.

> **THROUGHOUT WORLD WAR II THE ROYAL ARTILLERY WERE PROVIDED WITH AMMUNITION USED IN INFANTRY SUPPORT**

Military reports and requests for updated equipment, no doubt reinforced by one of Prime Minister Winston Churchill's famous 'Action this Day' directives, led to the development of the Featherstone factory, expanded by new buildings, as a site dedicated to providing the armed forces of the Crown with the most efficient tungsten-based armour-piercing ammunition the nation could provide. So it started and thus it continues.

Many of the existing buildings are the quickly run up flat roofed basic shells known to thousands of war workers, and both wartime, and post-war, National Service conscripts, as work place and home from home.

The Royal Ordnance as a civilian organisation under Army direction has a long and chequered history of providing firearms and ammunition of all calibres to the Army and latterly the Royal Navy. More recently in its post-war existence under the unified Ministry of Defence, which replaced the formerly separate, and sometimes uncooperative, Ministries of the three services, the RO has passed the

ammunition, of its own manufacturing to stringent quality controls, to the Royal Navy and Royal Marines, the Army and the Royal Air Force.

As a Government organisation the Royal Ordnance hired and still buys in manufacturing and management expertise by farming out much of its production to commercial companies; in this case to Hard Metal Tools Ltd of Coventry who were specialists in the production of steel alloys strengthened with the addition of expensive tungsten and other exotic minerals which vastly improve the qualities of common and cheaper steel. Throughout the period of hostilities Hard Metal Tools Ltd provided the expertise, gained in peacetime, to act as managing agent first for the Ministry of War and later for the post-war Ministry of Defence.

This was the common practice during World War Two when the new Ministry of Production was faced with the unique task of turning factories which had once produced peacetime essentials and luxuries into works which turned out high quality war material. Everyone concerned had to adapt to new jobs and working conditions, frequently exacerbated by the unwelcome attentions of enemy bombers dedicated to halting production. Civilians at home were often as much at war as many service men and women when working under enemy fire.

Featherstone set to on the manufacture of Small Arms Ammunition (SAA) providing .303 calibre cartridges, used in the excellent long-serving Lee-Enfield rifle known and trusted by millions of infantrymen and in the Czech-originated Bren gun.

The latter is an air cooled light machine gun, still in operational use, which is a delight both to fire and to maintain, a lovely reliable, trouble free platoon weapon operated by a two man crew. Here too were manufactured the vital tungsten-carbide 20 millimetre shells used by infantry and armoured vehicle heavy machine guns and in both fighter and bomber aircraft armament where soft-skinned lorries and aircraft and lightly armoured vehicles were the targets as much as the unknown chap on the other side who was shooting at you.

Throughout the war the Royal Artillery were provided with both six pounder and 17 pounder ammunition used in infantry support and against enemy infantry and armour. These traditional field piece shells were the mainstay of the Gunners' firepower for much of the war although other calibres and types of ammunition were produced elsewhere to provide for the inexhaustible requirements of the 'ubiquitous' Royal Regiment of Artillery.

Once peace was declared war production was run down as the enormous supplies of ammunition in daily use came to a full stop. Throughout the country staff who had enjoyed full employment with ample overtime suddenly found themselves relearning old, almost forgotten, skills as factories changed back to former peacetime production practices. The Royal Ordnance factories at Featherstone and elsewhere, which lived and

Above: Main Powder Processing Building 8F6 in the mid 1960s. This is now the main production building.

breathed on the production of war material, were unable to convert to making ploughshares, brassieres or confectionery etc. had no choice but to contract in size and reduce manpower to match loss of production. The post-war proliferation of little wars, revolutions and policing actions were yet to appear on the horizon of a world hungry for peace and a return to the half-remembered habits of peacetime.

By late 1947, during that icy winter of coal shortages at home when the Communists started a bitter civil war in Greece, Featherstone was manufacturing a new 20 pounder shell for the Royal Artillery. The new United Nations Organisation defence, between 1949 and 1951, of the Republic of Korea in which British forces were heavily committed against the invasion by Communist China called for supplies of 600,000 shells p.a. of this new shell alone. Such was the demand of this peace-keeping conflict that the 120 millimetre shell, another new item of artillery ammunition, was accelerated

forward from the experimental stage. Problems in firing the new round caused the new production line to be diverted to the production of the smaller, more effective, 90 millimetre (approximately 3 1/2 inches) HVAPUS armour-piercing round.

By 1956 development teams were working on the 105 millimetre APDS, which two years later evolved into model L28. This shell had an APDS core or explosive charge in the nose or 'bullet' part to provide the punch, allied with a tungsten alloy nose pad. This doggy term is the modern name for the tough armour-piercing cone, which sticks out like a bullet from its cartridge. The cartridge or shell case, formerly of brass and now of heat resistant plastic, is left behind when the bursting explosive forces the 'bullet' nose pad off on its rapid journey to its target.

DURING THE 1970s EXTRA MACHINES WERE INSTALLED TO INCREASE PRODUCTION

Above: Osmund 12 pipe Tungsten Reduction Furnace in 1977.

From this date onwards the old wartime standby of tungsten carbide cores were gradually replaced by the latest in weapon cores made from tungsten alloys now used in all ammunition made at Featherstone. The thrifty practice of recycling tungsten-based wastes from obsolescent stocks returned by the Forces, from its former tungsten carbide, current tungsten alloy and trimmed tungsten materials from the workshops has played a large part in enabling Featherstone to offer the MoD competitively priced products.

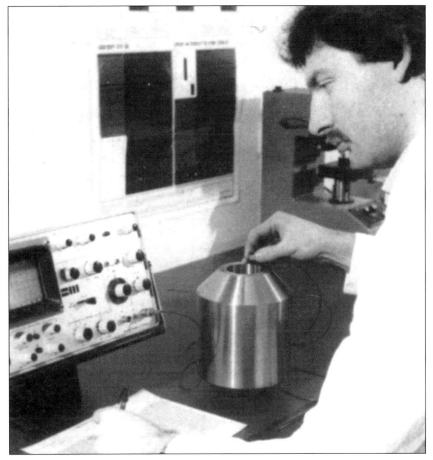

During post-war periods of retrenchment on defence budgets the armed forces of Britain have undergone drastic changes in expenditure on manning and equipment. Modern developments have played their part in both creating and adapting to these changes so that our slimmed-down services are indeed lean, keen and well equipped fighting machines run by departments who are as cost conscious as any civilian business. Today when the forces of allied nations cooperate in the exchange of military hardware it is essential that British manufacturers can compete to win orders from governments who may be impelled more by cost saving and international agreements than by patriotic or other reasons for buying from home manufacturers.

Changes in output were matched by changes in ownership as in 1963 Hard Metal Tools Ltd, the original agents running the plant for the Royal Ordnance since 1941, were transferred from the ownership of a firm of merchant bankers to that of the Wickman Organisation under the operational name of Wickman Wimet.

The low buildings at Featherstone housed the latest in Calcine and Hydrogen Pusher furnaces to process the raw materials into tough armour-piercing tungsten alloys.

Another new development of the era was the Dry and Wet Isostatic Pressing equipment used to form the cartridge. All meat and drink to the keen chemist of any age but rather mystifying to the layman who imagines ammunition to be put together rather in the manner of home-made fireworks or hand-filled shotgun cartridges.

Further changes occurred when the management of this government-owned

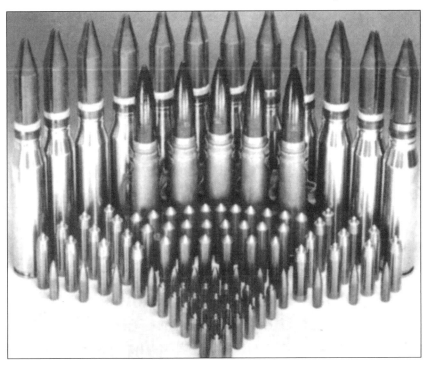

Above: Ultrasonic flaw detection - radiation shielding in the 1980s.
Left: A selection of APDS ammunition from 1980 - 1990.

ammunition factory run by operating agents Wickman Wimet passed, in 1973, into the hands of the Swedish company Sandvik AB. The new owners, from a neutral nation famed for the quality of its weapons, cars and cooking stoves, changed the name in 1976, to Wimet Ltd.

During the 1970s extra machines were installed to increase the production capacity to what it remains at to this day. This decade is fondly remembered as a period when 95 percent of output was sold to foreign clients buying British to equip their armed forces. The Royal Ordnance Factories won the Queen's Award for Industry thanks, in considerable part, to the success of the Featherstone works.

The successful 105 millimetre and 120 millimetre APDS shells continued in production as did new developments in ammunition for the splendid Chieftain tank and the amazing Harrier Jump-Jet hovering fixed wing aircraft. The self ranging 105 mm gun of the Chieftain brought a totally new concept of mobile artillery accuracy as the gun remained sighted on its target regardless of the undulations of the terrain or the tank's manoeuvre. The versatile Harrier, which requires no runway for taking off or landing on, has been adapted as a most useful offensive aircraft by all three services.

Modern ammunition has the appearance of weapons of the space age, once restricted to the realms of science fiction, in which we live today. Bullets and shells are now so advanced that they are called Kinetic Energy Penetrators. The output of the justifiably proud workforce of the Royal Ordnance Speciality Metals (ROSM) factory at Featherstone ranges from making such devices to providing 50% of the tungsten alloy used in darts for pubs, clubs and homes!

The plant's high quality tungsten alloys are now used in many civilian applications unlike the war materiel of the past. The medical world of hospital X-Ray departments has discarded heavy lead shields and aprons in favour of high density tungsten alloys to protect staff and patients from the incidence of X-Rays and Gamma-Rays used in radiography and treatment. Radioactive substances such as uranium and plutonium, used in nuclear power stations, are guarded both on site and in transit by shields and containers made of pressed and moulded tungsten alloys.

*Top: Wartime buildings used for powder production in the mid 1960s. **Above left:** Geofry Whitehouse OBE, Managing Director from the 1970s to the early 1980s.*

One of the latest developments is Tungsten Polymers. Even more flexible in production than previous products, these polymers can be injection-moulded just like any plastic bucket or toy. It follows that highly complex shapes can be moulded 'en masse' or individually at very cost effective prices.

Tungsten alloys are superior to any other known material for the precision balance weights needed to keep modern high technology measuring instruments on the ball. These are of particular value in the aerospace industry with its enormous requirements for balance weights in gyroscopes, computerised flight control systems and in balancing the finely tuned, yet sturdy, rotors of the immensely varied non fixed wing aircraft commonly called helicopters. Other uses for tungsten alloys between 0.5 grams and 100 kilograms in weight include underwater marine instruments such as cameras, tooling for drilling and industrial machines, and even high fidelity gramophones and music centres. Such fine engineering of precision made alloys can prevent the damaging vibration and chatter which reduces efficiency and increases costs in many machines with long shanks, axles or bearings.

From the early 1970s Wimet Ltd became managing agents to Royal Ordnance. The company was later privatised as RO Wimet with the Royal Ordnance holding 85 percent of the shares and Sandvik AB the remaining 15 percent.

During the half century or more that ammunition has been made at Featherstone over 20,000 tons of Tungsten products have been manufactured in competition with famous producers in France and Germany. Praise God and keep on passing the ammunition.

Below: The main powder production building in the mid 1980s. The prison farm is on the left. **Bottom:** *Present day main production building 8F6.*

Shopping for the twenty-first century

The Mander Centre is the lynch pin in the planners' concept of Wolverhampton as the designated sub-regional shopping entrepot for the counties of Shropshire, Stafford-shire, Worcestershire and the urban areas of the north western parts of the West Midlands. As the major town in the famous industrial area of the Black Country it proudly boasts a population rich in the skills which produced products exported to the ends of the earth together with a sense of humour and folklore second to none.

The prestigious five and a half acres, pedestrianised all weather shopping centre is widely regarded as the best in the region. It is positioned at the hub of the town centre as encircled by its wide ring road which provides easy access to out of town motorist and bus and train traveller alike. The two public transport stations and the well placed car parks help make shopping in both the town and the Centre a pleasure. The Mander Centre itself provides a comfortable and attractive link between traffic free Dudley Street and Victoria Street, both familiar to generations of Wolverhampton shoppers.

1965 saw the council, with remarkable foresight, approve plans to develop Wolverhampton in a style twenty years ahead of its rivals throughout the region. As, so often happens in rebuilding works

there have been contentious changes as old familiar buildings of comfortable scale gave way to a plainer style of architecture.

However human nature, even comedy, played its part in the development of the new enterprise when modern Irish navvies, finding gold under ground, immediately translated their treasure trove into good liquor with an alacrity which would have aroused the admiration of their forebears and descendants alike.

Below: The construction of the centre in 1964.
***Bottom:** The junction of Victoria Street and Bell Street in 1967.*

The Centre's first shop opened in the autumn of 1965 to be followed by Woolworth's and other High Street names once the Centre's teething troubles were resolved. These arose from problems in providing lavatories in sufficient number and suitable locations for public convenience. The newest lavatories provide both facilities for parents with babies and easy access for people with disabilities. Questions of ownership of rights of way and the huge needs for handy car parking facilities were ironed out in discussions with the council and neighbours.

The award of coveted Civic Trust accolades is highly satisfying to those who conceived and built the Mander Centre, without a penny piece of government funding. The visiting motorist is even happier knowing that their car is safely stowed in secured car parks which have won the equally valuable AA Gold Award for protected parking.

Since the Centre's 1987 refurbishment motorists can enjoy their trips between shops and car park in the scenic lifts which allow views over the town. Alternatively they can use the the four pairs of escalators, or moving staircases, which facilitate access between levels.Such access is a boon to the laden shopper with or without children.

Those who work in the offices of Mander House, which overlook the barrel arched conservatory roofs which allow light to enter the atrium below, can enjoy the best of working conditions coupled with access to all the facilities offered by the multi-faceted Mander centre. The present tenants include branches of famous outlets like Bhs, Tesco, Boots, WH Smith and TJ Hughes department store chain. The latter trades on four floors connected by escalators and stairs. Added to these are over 130 shops of varying sizes and contents to supplement those which have elected to continue trading in their traditional town centre locations.

The Mander story started in the late 1770s when Thomas Mander arrived in the small market town of Wolverhampton to make his fortune. The late Georgian era was one of enterprise and expansion as new ideas were in the air. The handsome, well proportioned houses and public buildings of the late Georgians reflect their personal financial successes and civic pride. Today their commodious and stylish homes are more often used as town centre offices by professional men and businesses.

The Mander Centre is something else and much more appropriate to our time. It was first developed by Manders in the mid-1960s, followed by additional phases in 1972 and 1976 and, most recently, refurbishment in 1987. The latter was as a result of the brave decision to spend £4M to upgrade the already award worthy standards to tempt the tenants to stay. In a period of downturn of retail trading throughout the West

Left: Mander Square before refurbishment.

family firm, is now a deservedly popular hotel, famed throughout the Black Country.

Even well established businesses have to change and expand into new fields as the Manders did in the late 1960s and 70s. To the people of the Black Country, and its enormous trading and shopping hinterland, the most visible, prestigious and popular element of Mander success is that quarter of Wolverhampton known as the Mander Centre. Bounded by Queen's Square, Victoria Street, Dudley Street and Bell Street this modern concept embodies one stop, all weather under cover shopping convenience and choice.

This imaginative and visually exciting project progressed in liaison with the original architects included the fabulous, handsomely barrel vaulted, sliding roof of ten parts. Once the former open square had been converted to a protected atrium, which enjoyed the extra benefit of hot weather opening, it greatly extended the potential of this space.

The Mander Centre now has a multi-use Exhibition Area, with easy access for exhibitor and public alike, which has frequently been used for promenade concerts for up to 800 music lovers. Wolverhampton can be proud of this latest addition to its rich cultural heritage so easily available to the busy people of the region as we reach into the twenty first century.

Midlands this bold step has locally reversed the trend in that the renewed Mander Centre is as attractive to the retailers, who have filled every shop, as to the shoppers who alone turn it into the commercial success which local people have come to expect of the name Manders.

Wightwick Manor, built on paint and chemicals, a former Mander home now in the hands of the National Trust, was one of the pioneers in having electric lighting and purpose built bathrooms and other wonders of the Industrial Age when architects were even installing lifts and the first central heating since the Romans. The Mount at Tettenhall, another Mander mansion built on the profits of the

Above: The Fountain area and scenic lifts which replaced the pram ramp.
Top: Mander Square, main area.

Neither the tenants nor the shoppers were inconvenienced throughout the 15 months of extensive alterations. Unusually in the world of public works no alteration work was done on Saturdays nor in the 1986 Christmas shopping period. For the Mander Centre it was a time of business as usual in the best traditions of Britons under fire. We are, after all, a nation of shopkeepers.

This great shopping centre occupies a site once home to the elegant Central Arcade, which was burnt out in the 1970s and the well loved and sadly missed Star and Garter, a former coaching inn.

Earlier Mander involvement in the site was once vividly present in the form of the Paint Works from whose interesting odours residents could tell the direction of the wind. The other redolent local guides to wind direction included the slaughter-house and one other site which the older reader will remember.

The Mander Centre Tower provides prestigious offices for many local firms who value a prime city centre location with car parks, catering, shopping

and recreation facilities on site for both their staff and for their clients. Mander Shopping, as the Centre is locally known, enables men, women and children to buy clothing from head to foot, arrange their holidays and look after their health and wealth. The Centre's commitment to a safe and happy shopping experience is backed by state of the art CCTV and fire control systems.

Having enjoyed snacks or meals shoppers may patronise retailers of audio-visual equipment, electrical and automobile accessories before watching displays in the covered open spaces. DIY and sports enthusiasts are well catered for while passers by can purchase smokers' requisites, books and journals. Shoppers may find jobs, toys, games and crafts while even pets are not neglected in the diversity of shopping facilities. All this in elegant surroundings enhanced by Italianate marble floors, new stainless steel and glass protective balustrading and improved lighting. The epitome of the twenty first century shopping environment.

Left: Victoria Arcade.
Below: An aerial view of the Centre today.

Helpers of the blind

The Blind Persons Act was passed in 1920 and was the first legislation which obliged Local Authorities to provide welfare for the blind, but the people of Wolverhampton had pre-empted this Act by some 45 years. Mrs E A Whitehouse of Parkdale, Wolverhampton, had raised the sum of £50 and in 1875, with the help of friends, founded an organisation known as the Wolverhampton Society for the (Outdoor) Blind. The Society's first mission was to visit blind people in the area and give them an opportunity to learn to read; all those who wished to learn, and were able to, were taught to decipher embossed type. The Society's activities extended over Wolverhampton, Bilston, Willenhall, Wednesfield, Penn, Wombourne and Tettenhall, and in the whole of this area there were 93 known blind people.

The Society first became involved in the provision of employment for blind people in 1882, acquiring a house in Alexandra Street where five blind men could work, and in 1889 new workshops were opened in John Street by the Earl and Countess of Dartmouth. By then the Society also had a workshop and retail outlet at 17a Victoria Street, where baskets, chair seating and mats were woven and sold. Fifteen men and three women were employed on this venture.

By 1920 the area covered had been extended to include the whole of Seisdon and Dudley, and in 1924 the Society moved out of Alexandra Street, Victoria Street and John Street and into Douro House at 62 Waterloo Road, which provided workshops, offices and recreation rooms. Its shop had moved to 45 Lichfield Street, and the following year it moved again, to 13 Central Arcade. The Society's name was altered in 1926 to the Wolverhampton, Dudley and Districts Institution for the Blind, to reflect its increased area of operations, and a shop was opened in Dudley, at 197 High Street, in 1928. Throughout all these developments Mrs Whitehouse had remained a Committee member and had taken an active interest in the Society's work; but, having seen the Society's good work expand into the Dudley area, Mrs Whitehouse sadly passed away in 1929.

For the next decade and during the war years the Institution embarked on few new ventures; it did, however, establish a Building Fund, recognising that its current headquarters and workshops would soon become inadequate for its growing needs. The National Assistance Act of 1948 restated the provisions of the 1920 Blind Persons Act, and it also defined blindness and instituted a register of blind and of partially sighted persons. The maintenance of the register was the responsibility of local authorities. In fact, since the

Above: A Report dating from 1914 on the actions and activities of the centre.
Left: Carpet weaving in the 1950s.

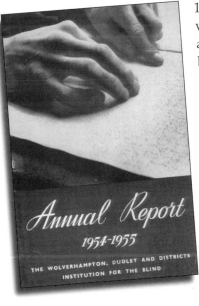

1920 Act many local voluntary societies and institutions had become agents of the Authorities with the duties of discharging the statutory functions, but the Wolverhampton, Dudley and Districts Institution for the Blind had remained in the hands of its Trustees. In 1961, however, it became an Incorporated body governed by a Council of Management, which consisted of elected members and Local Authority representatives. It also changed its name to the Wolverhampton, Dudley and Districts Institute for the Blind.

At around this time the Building Fund, which had attracted generous public support, was able to purchase seven acres of land at Sedgley from the Earl of Dudley with a view to building a new Welfare Centre. This was opened in January 1963; facilities include a concert hall, canteen, handicraft room, Braille library, offices, and a large single storey building containing workshops. The total cost of the project was

£200,000; grants towards the workshops were received from the local authorities and the Ministry of Labour.

During the second half of the 1960s, a number of initiatives led to reorganisation of workshop employment for the blind. Two of the Sedgley

Above: Basket Weaving was taught as a trade.
Above left: The 1954-55 Institution Report.
Top: A day trip organised in the 1950s to Rhyl.

The Institute now set up another fund, this time for the purpose of building and equipping a residential home. The nearest homes for the blind were in the Birmingham area at Erdington, or many miles north at Stoke-on-Trent, and over the years there had been been a growing feeling that residential accommodation should be provided for the local blind population. This project came to fruition in March 1973 with the opening of Beacon House at Sedgley, a fine modern building providing accommodation for approximately 40 blind men and women. The vast majority of the residents are elderly, and the well-planned, well-equipped facilities mean that they can now receive every possible care and attention. The total cost of the project was around £120,000, and funding for the running costs comes partly from local authorities who sponsor admissions, and partly from the Institute's general funds.

workshops were used to provide sighted disabled people with employment in the engineering field, marking the creation of the Industries for the Blind and Disabled in 1965; the following year further re-organisation resulted in the development of engineering work in place of the traditional crafts. This led to the closure of the Institute's two shops, as the goods now being produced were not suitable for retail sale; the Dudley shop closed in 1966, while the Wolverhampton shop managed to stay open until 1968.

Above: Group Captain Douglas Bader visits the workshops in 1965.
Below: HRH Duchess of Kent officially opening the day centre on the 31st October 1973.

The next addition to the Institute's amenities was the Day Centre, which opened in August 1973. Situated in one of the workshops which was specially converted for the purpose, the Centre includes a reading room, a work area, a hairdressing salon, workstations for tuition in Braille and typing, workspace for pottery and woodwork, and a kitchen and living room where domestic skills can be learned and practised. The Centre is attended by well over 100 visually impaired people who are brought in on various days by the Institute's transport service, and social workers from Wolverhampton and Dudley join the Institute staff in organising projects and conducting training courses, including mobility instruction.

As the welfare amenities at Sedgley developed and became the focus of activities for the local blind population, it became desirable to provide accommodation on the site so that blind men and women who had no need of residential care could have daily access to the various services which the Institute provided. The Institute therefore prepared to begin raising funds again, this time in order to build a number of bungalows on the site. It was expected that this would be a long-term project, as it would have taken many years to accumulate the necessary capital; however, through the generosity of Wolverhampton-born industrialist Sir Charles Hayward who offered to fund the whole of the construction costs from the Hayward Foundation,

this ambitious scheme became reality very quickly. Thanks to Sir Charles' magnificent gesture, work began immediately and 33 blind tenants were able to move into the 27 purpose-built bungalows much sooner than had originally been hoped.

To reflect the changing circumstances the Institute became Beacon Centre for the Blind in 1991, and will continue to provide services to blind and partially sighted people into the next millennium.

Top: Sir Charles Hayward at the opening of the bungalows in 1976.
Below: An aerial view of the Beacon Centre for the Blind.

Keeping the motorist on the road

When Bernard Littleford left the Sunbeam Motor Company in Wolverhampton in 1923 to start up his own garage business, he little knew how far his fledgling company was to eventually go.

The years of the second world war were not easy for those businesses involved in the motor trade. The chronic shortage of parts, petrol rationing, and the almost total absence of new cars (Vauxhall only produced around 100 cars between 1939 and 1946) all combined to make things difficult for garage owners. Even towards the end of the 1940s the effects of the war were still being felt, and certain goods remained in short supply. This included the motor car, as new cars were being exported as fast as they came off the production line.

Right: The L-Type was the first post war Vauxhall to be launched in October 1948.
Below: The Victor - launched in 1958.

Though Britain still had a long way to go before post-war prosperity became a reality (a car was an unattainable dream for the average family), there were still a large number of mostly pre-war cars about, and Bernard Littleford was perceptive enough to recognise the enormous potential of the motor car as the vehicle of the future. The business survived the difficult times and looked hopefully towards the future.

Originally located in the Chapel Ash area, over the years the company held a wide variety of franchises which have included Armstrong Siddeley, Singer and the Rootes range which eventually became part of the Chrysler organisation. In 1982 the opportunity came to take up the prestigious Vauxhall dealership.

Continued expansion and development called for larger premises, and in 1965 a move was made to the firm's current premises in Bilston Road. Quality Manager Clive Dunn remembers that move well; his involvement with the Vauxhall Dealership C D Bramall began more than 30 years ago in 1962. Since then Clive has held a number of positions within the company, including that of Bodyshop Manager. Today, as part of the Management Team, he ensures that the strict quality standards required by government legislation are met as well as the requirements of the Group - and of course, those of Vauxhall themselves.

Four years on further land was acquired to allow more space for the company's expanding used car sales business. A little later a large bodyshop was built.

C D Bramall's Vauxhall Dealership Director is Derek Wheeler, who took on the responsibility back in 1976. The years from the 1970s to the present day have seen vast changes and developments, and Derek has been

there to see them all. He well remembers the key development that took place in 1986, when the company was acquired by the C D Bramall organisation - one of the largest dealer groups in the country. The dramatic changes that took place within the motor retail industry called for a dedicated workforce to consolidate the growing business, and the firm's competent team more than fits the bill. A large number of today's workforce have been with the company for many years.

The Dealership's main site at Bilston Road encompasses all the retail activity. The sale of new and used vehicles, the comprehensive servicing and repair shop and the bodyshop, as well as a large parts operation, are all situated at the Bilston Road premises. A support facility on a separate site deals with the storing and preparing of new and used vehicles.

With an eye to new innovations and franchising arrangements, the new year of 1998 was ushered in with the acquisition of Worfield Garage on the Bridgnorth Road, which now proudly bears the title C D Bramall Worfield, and has a staff of twenty. A subsidiary of CD Bramall Wolverhampton, the long-established site had for many years handled the sales and servicing of Vauxhall vehicles.

Above: From the mid 1950s minor changes were being made to the E-Types, with the fronts being altered.

It is, of course, the quality of the product that spells success or failure for a business, and Vauxhall has for many years been at the cutting edge of the latest technology. From the production of the first Vauxhall motor car in 1903 the company has continued to turn out an exceptional product, only slowing their production of private cars during the second world war to concentrate on Luton-built Bedford trucks for the services, jet aircraft engines, highly secret work on mines, torpedoes and other weapons, and on the spectacular Churchill tank. Normally it would take around four years to produce such a vehicle, yet the 38-ton Churchill tank was designed and built by Vauxhall within twelve months - an incredible feat.

The Bilston Road site itself has gone through many changes and developments over the years until today a workforce of 120 is employed on the premises to cover the many differing aspects of the trade, from the courteous sales force who deal with both new and used vehicles to the skilled mechanics who repair and service private cars and vans.

Above left: Used car display in the early 1970s.
Top: The Littleford showroom as it appeared in the early 1970s.

Normal production at Vauxhall resumed in 1946, and it says much for the company that only three years later an incredible 55,000 Vauxhall Tens had been built! For Vauxhall, the 1950s was a decade of maximum expansion, with a massive demand for their distinctive vehicles. Who can forget those marvellous 50s vehicles? The Victor, which became Britain's number one export car; the Victor estate; the successful E-type Wyvern, Velox and Cresta, replaced in 1957 by the long and sleek PA Sixes....

An influx of new models marked the 1960s and 70s, notably the immensely popular Chevette, the Cavalier, the Carlton and late in the decade the Royale. The millionth Viva came off the production line in 1971. The year 1980 ushered in the Astra - a product to be proud of, and one which has remained high on the popularity list at Bilston Road to the present day.

The satisfaction of the client is of major importance to C D Bramall, and over the years they have built up a reputation as a company with a high level of customer care. Derek Wheeler puts this down first of all to the way that the staff are treated. A satisfied workforce is pivotal to the smooth running of the business, and he firmly believes that a workforce who are treated well will in turn treat clients in the same way.

The team at C D Bramall believe that the Vauxhall dealership is one of which they can be justifiably proud. The Vauxhall product range covers all aspects of motoring and has a vehicle to suit the needs of every driver, from the Astra and the economical Corsa to the medium-range Vectra and the popular Omega.

Tapping into a wide range of technical innovation, Vauxhall is part of General Motors, the largest vehicle motor manufacturer in the world, and their role in the worldwide organisation has helped to develop the Vauxhall product into the sophisticated range that it is today. Vauxhall has continually remained at the forefront of innovation within motor manufacture, and their fine products have won through to remain high in the popularity stakes with the discriminating motorists of the late 20th century.

Above: The CD Bramall showroom in modern times.
Below: Derek Wheeler - Dealership Director.

Achievement through caring

The first of April, 1850 was a significant day for the children of Wolverhampton, and not simply because of the practical jokes which they might have looked forward to playing on each other. An event happened on that date which was to make a difference to the lives of generation after generation of Wolverhampton youngsters, giving them more opportunities, brighter futures, and all the other advantages which a good education brings with it. The event was the establishment of an orphanage at 46 Queen Street, Wolverhampton; and it is from that same charitable foundation that The Royal Wolverhampton School has grown.

The man responsible for the foundation of the Wolverhampton Orphanage was John Lees, a former lock and key manufacturer who had later become a hardware factor and merchant. The Trustees of the orphanage also included his brother Richard, nephew William, and great-nephews Lawrence and Eustace, all of whom also served on the Board of Governors, and in fact records of the Trustees show that four generations

of the family were involved, concluding with John Lees' great-great-niece. The aim which the original Trustees worked towards was the provision of an education for children between the ages of seven and fourteen. However, it soon became apparent that the premises at Queen Street would not be large enough to continue to fulfil their purpose for long, and one of their first challenges, therefore, was to raise the capital to finance the construction of new buildings for the orphanage. They succeeded in doing this in a remarkably short space of time. The sum of £7,000 was raised entirely from voluntary subscriptions, and the new orphanage at Goldthorn Hill was opened on 25 June 1854.

Today, in the elegant, ivy-clad building of The Royal Wolverhampton School, set in tranquil surroundings along Penn Road, the tradition which was established almost a century and a half ago continues, ensuring that the young people entrusted to its care are given the best possible start in life. Awarded its Royal patronage by Queen Victoria in 1891 in commemoration of 40 years of work with children in need, the School now caters for children between the ages of two and 18, providing a continuous education for boys and girls from nursery to sixth form.
Pupils living in Wolverhampton and

Above: The school building and playing fields circa 1900.
Above left: The 'Long Dorm' circa 1900.
Left: A classroom circa 1900.

by an efficient management structure firmly committed to a policy of combining quality with value for money, which means that the School's fees have been kept well within the lower third of the market range. A significant number of Merit Scholarships are also available, including bursaries and Orphan Foundation Awards. Donations and bequests to be used towards the future provision of bursaries and scholarships or towards the development of the School are always welcome.

the West Midlands can attend the School as day pupils, and boarding places are available to children of service families as well as at the Orphan Foundation. Also on the School's register are a number of students from other countries including Germany, Hong Kong, mainland China, Taiwan, Thailand, Korea, Malaysia and Singapore, so that from an early age all the children have the opportunity to share valuable insights into other cultures.

The Royal Wolverhampton School has a wide range of modern facilities and equipment, including a 25m indoor swimming pool. It has built up an excellent track record of achieving good examination results, and has a particularly strong reputation in the fields of Music and the Sciences. Parents who are considering sending their children to the Royal Wolverhampton School are pleasantly surprised to discover that the high standard of education provided is complemented

The most valuable gift a child can receive is a good education, and the Royal Wolverhampton School makes it possible for children of proven academic ability to receive an education of the very highest standard, in spite of parental circumstances if needs be. For this, thanks must go to John Lees, the founder; to the people of Wolverhampton whose generosity funded the original building work; and to all those whose tireless efforts have helped The Royal Wolverhampton School and its Orphan Foundation achieve the high standards for which it is recognised today.

Top: The Queen Mother's visit to the school in 1969 to open the dining room and science block in the senior school. She is the school's patron.
Above left: A classroom circa 1999. French is taught from age three years.
Below: The school building today.

S & J Dixon & Son Ltd - More than a century's experience in meeting the decorator's needs

Can you imagine your home without wallpaper? In fact, although wallpaper first appeared in Europe in the 16th century, it was not until the continuous printing process was introduced in the 1830s that wallpaper became a common feature in houses. So the wallpaper shop on the corner of Bennetts Hill and New Street, Birmingham in the early 1850s, where a young man named Joseph Dixon was employed, must have been one of the first shops of its kind in Birmingham. In 1854 Joseph left the shop to set up in business on his own account, visiting local builders with his sample book of wallpapers which he had bought direct from the manufacturer; his enterprise paid off and within a few years he was able to open his own shop.

In 1880 he opened a second shop, to be run by his son Samuel, in the Gas Office Buildings in Darlington Street, Wolverhampton. The London Paperhanging Stores, as it was called up until 1944, stocked a wide range of wallpapers from the newest designs in French good satin papers from 9d a piece to patterns for small houses from 2d a piece. It also sold cigars.

The entire business was transferred to Samuel in the mid 1880s when Joseph Dixon emigrated to America.

Samuel stopped selling cigars; also, more significantly, he tired of being asked by customers if he could recommend a good decorator, and began to employ men to hang the wallpaper he sold. His workforce grew to around 60, and included plumbers; and for a time contracting was an important facet of the business.

Samuel was joined in the business in 1921 by his 17 year old son Leslie, who proved to be a dynamic force; it was at his suggestion that the company purchased its first motor vehicle, a Ford Model T van, and it was he who persuaded his father to form a Limited Company, which was effected in 1935. At this point Wolverhampton was well established as the Head Office of the Company.

Paint had by this time become an important part of the business; at first all paint was mixed by the decorator, but by the early 1930s ready mixed paint had come onto the market, and in the mid 30s the company developed its own brand of paint, sold as Dixolin at 7s 8d a gallon. When war broke out, however, paint became scarce; the company bought all it could, and managed to maintain supplies to its customers throughout the war.

The Company celebrated its Centenary in 1954 with a memorable evening of dancing and entertainment at the Civic Hall, with a buffet and free drinks for customers, suppliers and staff.

Above: An advertisement circa 1890.
Top left: Joseph Dixon, the company's founder. Left: Staff outside the entrance in the late 1930s after a fire ravaged the building.

The staff at this time numbered around 50, a lively set of characters, many of whom had been with the company for a long time, and who enthusiastically joined in Company social events and outings; the Annual Dinner Dance tradition, established in 1947, is an important feature on the Company calendar.

Shortly after its Centenary, the company began to expand its retail activities. A branch was opened in Stoke in 1958, followed by one in Sutton in 1962 and one in Bridgnorth in 1967, and by 1978 there were in excess of 20 branches across the West Midlands. However, at a policy review in 1978 it was decided that Trade business should remain the company's main focus.

By 1979 Dixons was operating from 17 branches, and there had been considerable development of its trade depots. The Company marked its 125th Anniversary with a series of major promotions and events for customers and suppliers, bonuses and gifts for staff, and a fundraising drive which raised some £5,000 towards equipment for disabled children - and, of course, a very special Dinner Dance. In 1991, Dixon's acquired its local competitor, Decorarte Lovett, who had six outlets, thus acquiring a second Wolverhampton branch at Chapel Ash.

Today, S J Dixon, under the Chairmanship of Brian Dixon (fourth generation), has 19 branches in the West and East Midlands which stock paint, wall covering, fabric and ancillary products to meet all the decorative needs of the traditional decorator, the independent retailer and the general public. Customers include retail Superstores, local authorities

and decorating companies both large and small. These customers rely on the first class, personal service of Dixon's well-informed and experienced staff, backed by a modern computer system which provides a rapid response to queries, and also supports a distribution service providing next day delivery of wallcoverings to retailers. It has always been Dixon's policy to recognise the importance of staff and their need to enjoy their working environment, and the company has succeeded in retaining a family atmosphere throughout its growth and development. Plans for the future include consolidating and expanding its branch network within the greater Midlands area, maintaining its traditional base in Wolverhampton, enhancing its position as a leading national distributor - and enjoying many more anniversary celebrations!

Above: The annual staff dinner dance in January 1953.
Below: The made-to-measure fabric department in the early 1980s.

Arthur M Griffiths & Son Ltd celebrate their centenary

It is impossible to travel far in the vicinity of Wolverhampton without passing a building constructed by Arthur M Griffiths and Son Ltd. Drive across from the east and see Tamworth College of Further Education and Tamworth Probation Unit; come through Stafford and admire the Trinity Methodist Church; approach from the south, and you can pass Wednesfield High School. Much of the housing on the outskirts of Wolverhampton was built by Arthur M Griffiths, including the Low Hill estate and the private developments at Fallings Park and Penn. And in Wolverhampton itself, Arthur M Griffiths & Son Ltd's buildings abound: the Staffordshire Building Society by the ring road, the YWCA Hostel on Penn Road, Penn Road Surgery and the Buddha Temple.

A century ago, however, Arthur M Griffiths had no plans to build a temple. A carpenter by trade, he had set up in business as a jobbing builder, working from a small shed in Church Lane. Five years later he moved round the corner to Thomas Street, where in due course he was joined by his son Harry. By this time Arthur was building and selling new houses, and he and his son were able to develop the business so that by the 1930s they were able to take on Local Authority

contracts to build council houses in Wolverhampton, Coseley, Stourbridge, Wednesfield and the surrounding areas. The construction of 500 homes at Low Hill was one of their first major contracts.

In 1934 the firm moved to new offices, and during the war years they were employed mostly on factory maintenance and government work. The shortage of skilled craftsmen meant long working hours to maintain the first class service and reliability upon which the firm's reputation depended. By the end of the war they were firmly established as an experienced and reliable company, and the post war years brought them contracts to build schools for Salop and Staffordshire County Councils and Wolverhampton and Dudley Borough

Above: An aerial view of the early days.
Top: Reflecting the past from the turn of the century.
Left: Digging a new press base - Rubery Owen, Darleston.

Councils, and hospitals for area health authorities and the West Midlands Regional Health Authority. Since then the list of public buildings built by the company has continued to grow, to include the lecture theatre and Medical Centre at New Cross Hospital, West Park Hospital, Compton Hospice, Parkfield Mentally Handicapped Unit and Wolverhampton Borough Council's new Cemetery buildings. Major projects carried out for private developers have included factory extensions for Howard Perry, a transport office and workshop for R and M Shorthouse, and a factory and office block for Davenport Burgess. One of the more unusual jobs which the firm has undertaken is the restoration of Oxley House, a 19th century mansion in Wolverhampton which had been gutted by fire. Arthur M Griffiths and Son Ltd was commissioned by the Heantun Housing Association to restore the structure and convert it into housing; the work took a year to complete, and cost £400,000.

However, the company's involvement in prestigious landmark ventures does not mean that it no longer has time for the individual whose requirements are on a much smaller scale. The small works division attaches just as much importance to building a kitchen extension or even repairing a leaky roof, and all customers receive the same personal attention.

The company has kept abreast of developments, both in the area of new material technology and in the computer systems which it uses, but it has not lost sight of the value of traditional craftsmanship. It prefers to carry out all aspects of the work in-house to its own high standards rather than sub-contract; bricklaying, carpentry, plastering, painting and plumbing are amongst the skills of its workforce, and it is one of the few building companies which still has its own joinery shop. The company has a staff of almost a hundred, and each worker is a

valued member of the team, many of them remaining with the firm throughout their working lives and becoming 'part of the family'. Over the years more than 100 employees have been presented with gold watches in recognition of 25 years service. It is the Company's policy to look after its staff from the moment they join.

All these factors have played a part in the success of the family firm which has built Wolverhampton, but perhaps most important of all is the firm's pride in its work and its commitment to giving satisfaction to every single customer, no matter how large or small.

Above right: Arthur M Griffiths' offices today. From left to right: Alan Griffiths, Elizabeth Gutteridge, Maurice Walsh and Simon Dix. Above left: The offices occupied by the company until 1998. Below: The machinery and technology of today producing fine quality windows. Also the company still uses traditional skills to produce products.

The Wolverhampton Metal Company Ltd - 95 years of ingotmaking and metal reclamation

Sadly, 1998 will mark the end of 95 years of ingot-making and metal recla-mation in Wolverhampton.

The Wolverhampton Metal Company Ltd was incorporated in 1903, when it moved to the site in Well Lane, Wednesfield, which in December 1998 it still occupies. Its founder, Henry B Summerhill, had by that time acquired some 20 years experience of metal merchanting, having switched his trade from that of agricultural merchant to metal merchant in the early 1880s.

The principles upon which his new business was based were in many ways very much in line with 1990s thinking, being essentially concerned with recycling: lead and zinc scraps and residues were processed back into useable ingot form. The process was simple: the factory was equipped with simple 160lb coke-fired pot furnaces, and the scraps and residues were delivered to the factory in sacks, sorted into grades and then melted in the furnaces to produce molten metal, which was then poured into ingot form and sold. Sales in the early

days of the business began around five tonnes a week, and were gradually built up to several hundred tonnes a week; the best ever weekly sales figure was 800 tonnes, which was achieved during the 1970s.

The owners then began to develop new furnacing methods to deal with low grade scraps, exploring, for instance, the use of reverbatory furnaces, and they had to overcome many teething problems before achieving success.

Lead and zinc, and later brass and gunmetal, were processed. The wars, of course, gave great impetus

Left: Henry B. Summerhill. **Below:** *Scrap being sorted into grades.* **Bottom:** *Reverbatory furnace - pouring ingots by hand using ladles.*

to scrap recovery and reclamation and helped the company to grow; although it also threatened to put an end to the factory altogether, as the site was noted on a Luftwaffe map as a bomb target in the second world war. Fortunately, it was never hit. The company's post-wartime salvage activities included stripping down for scrap the warship HMS Warspite, famous for its role in the Battle of the River Plate. The huge ship ran aground while being towed to the scrap yard and had to be dismantled just off the beach at St. Michaels Mount. After the war, the company was able to expand its operations and it purchased a fleet of lorries which were used for collecting scraps and distributing ingot around the UK.

New techniques in copper refining meant that more alloys could be produced, and the company began to concentrate on copper alloy ingots which, because of their special qualities, are very resistant to attack from water and weathering. Brass, which is a copper alloy, is used for making taps, and gunmetal is used to manufacture valves; aluminium bronze for ships' propellors became the company's main export. The growth of the copper residue business led to the purchase of James Bridge, which is now the UK's only copper refinery. Over the years the company built up a reputation for supplying high quality ingot, and for the technical support which it was able to give to its customers both at home and abroad. Customers were mainly foundries casting metal components in specification copper alloys, and included tap manufacturers, ships' propellors casters, copper billet producers, copper alloy rod producers and valve manufacturers.

From the founding of the business until the mid 1980s, when the last member of the founder's family retired, three generations of the family have run the company. Henry B Summerhill was joined on the

Top left: HMS Warspite, *stripped down by the company for scrap.* *Top right:* The company's fleet in the 1950s. *Right:* Colonel FW James *who retired in 1985. He was the third generation of the family to run the business.*

Board in 1903 by six grandsons, each of whom had their own specific management role: H S James was responsible for sales and works management, sharing responsibility for sales with H V James; P A James was Secretary; W R James was an Analytical Chemist; F S James developed copper refining; and T C James' role was in general management. The family tradition came to an end with the retirement of F W James, known as Walter, great grandson of the founder.

Throughout its 95 years in the business, the Wolverhampton Metal Company Ltd remained at the same premises, where a comparison between the original pot furnaces which were used in 1903 and the two tonne coreless electric induction furnaces and ten tonne rotary oil fired furnace which stand there today gives an indication of the progress which has taken place over the years.

When the Wolverhampton Metal Company ceases trading at the end of 1998, five copper alloy ingot-makers will remain in the UK, with twenty plus in Europe, mainly in Germany and Italy. At the end of the second world war, there were up to forty such companies in the UK alone.

It is always sad when a company ceases to exist; but the Wolverhampton Metal Company can look back with pride over a long and successful history, the result of the skill and hard work of three generations of the founder's family.

A personal, caring and quality service provided by five generations of a family firm

Mr George Jennings, the founder of Jennings Funeral Directors, was born in 1826. He was a woodworker and craftsman by trade, working from Union Mill Street, Wolverhampton, until a close family friend came to him with the request that he undertake a funeral for them.

George Jennings obliged, and it can be assumed that all went smoothly on that first occasion because in 1848 George and his wife Sarah set up in business as Undertakers at the same premises in Union Mill Street. The chief focus of the Funeral Furnishing Establishment, as it was termed on the early Company letterhead, was coffin-making and general undertaking. With Sarah Jennings taking charge of the administration of the business and other aspects of the undertaking work, the couple employed no outside help, preferring to do every-thing themselves; this sometimes meant working through the night, but it also meant that they learned, first-hand, everything there was to know about the profession. Their reputation soon became established as they won the confidence of the local people. Meanwhile, their son Frederick had joined his parents in the family business and was learning from them the skills involved in funeral direction. In 1875 George Jennings handed the business over to his son, and he and Sarah were then able to enjoy a well-earned retirement until 1907, the year in which they both died.

The property at Union Mill Street provided limited accommodation which was barely adequate now that the business had grown, and Frederick's first major business decision was to acquire new premises in St James' Street. This gave him better facilities, including a coach-house and

Above: Brothers George and Frederick Jennings (Jnr), pictured at Merridale Cemetery in 1919.
Top left: George Jennings, founder of the company.
Left: Frederick Jennings Snr (front right) with Jack Jennings sitting beside him, pictured in 1910.

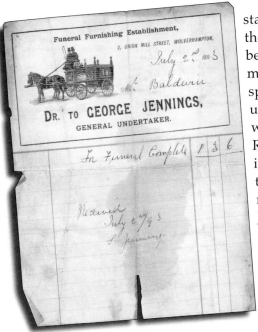

stabling for the horses, besides much more space to set up modern workshops. Records indicate that the move to St James' Street took place between 1893 and 1903. Frederick Jennings continued to run the firm, now known as F Jennings and Sons, until his death in 1916, when his three sons, Frederick Jnr, George and John (known as Jack) inherited the business. Jack chose not to follow in what had now become established as the family footsteps, and instead joined the Methodist Ministry after leaving H M Forces, whilst Frederick and George took charge jointly, pursuing their father's moves towards extending the facilities available to relatives of the deceased by purchasing and refurbishing adjacent property in Horseley Field. A Service Chapel, panelled in oak, was built on the premises, as were three Rest Chapels with leaded windows, of which one symbolised 'The Light of the World', another 'Crown of Life' and the third 'The Resurrection'. These were completed by 1937. Further improvements were carried out to the offices, reception rooms, workshops and garage; the period between the wars had also seen the introduction of a fleet of motor vehicles, which included the Model 'T' Ford, to replace the horse-drawn hearses and carriages. It is recorded that the firm bought its first Daimlers very soon after the end of the second world war, from the Royal Mews at Buckingham Palace. Another intriguing piece of Second World War documentation which the firm has kept on file is a letter giving permission to enter Coventry with coffins, following the air raids.

At the time of the firm's celebration of its Centenary in 1948, the third and fourth generations of the family were working together, with Frederick and George having been joined in the

1930s by sons George Jnr, John and Harold Jennings. Under their management, facilities were improved still further with the construction of St James' House, which is amongst the finest Funeral Homes in the country, and contains 14 individual Chapels of Rest which provide a peaceful setting, appropriate to any religion and culture, where people who were close to the deceased may spend time in quiet reflection.

The current Directors of F Jennings, brothers David and Philip and cousin Roger, represent the fifth generation of the Jennings family. Ever sensitive to the needs of those they serve, these five generations have, between them, guided the firm through many changes: from horse-drawn hearses and the small cottage property in Union Mill Street where the founder and his wife, working day and night, attained standards which met and surpassed the expectations of the community in which they lived, to modern, comfortable limousines, a tastefully-appointed Funeral Home with extensive facilities, and a wide range of complementary services, from repatriation to ordering floral tributes - again, meeting and surpassing the more complex expectations of today's bereaved. The personal, caring and quality service provided by this family business has helped many thousands of local families in their times of loss, and will continue to do so for many generations yet to come.

Above: An invoice issued in 1893 for funeral expenses.
Right: The Jennings premises in July 1964.

The Heart Of Shopping In Wolverhampton

First there was a rumour, and people's hopes began to rise; then it was official, and the news gladdened the hearts of Wolverhampton's shoppers: the Wulfrun shopping centre was to be given a facelift, and work was scheduled to start in late August 1998.

As many of these shoppers will remember, the Wulfrun Centre was built between 1966 and 1969, in two phases. Each phase was greeted with tremendous enthusiasm; situated off Dudley Street and extremely convenient for the bus station, the new Centre introduced an increasing number of the big-name chain stores to Wolverhampton, and brought the latest in 60s and 70s fashion, entertainment and novelty goods within reach. Equally, its paved areas with seating and landscaping features made it a pleasant place to spend time, strolling up and down the arcades, stopping for a snack and a chat with friends, and returning for another leisurely spell of window-shopping before making the final decision on the day's purchases. The Centre's popularity lasted for many years, but inevitably it began to show its age. As the 80s turned into the 90s and new concepts in shopping centre design were developed, the Wulfrun Centre's open walkways and concrete facades began to look dated. Because of its prime location, the Centre has managed to trade successfully, but it is a long time since it excited shoppers; this, however, is about to change.

In August 1998 work began on a 13-month project to revitalise the Wulfrun Centre. The refurbishment

scheme has been planned by London and Cambridge Properties, who purchased the centre in 1994. In drawing up the plans, LCP has worked closely with the council, and has used the services of international architects Chapman Taylor Partners. The Centre will remain open throughout the construction period, and much of the work will be carried out at night, in order to minimise disruption for both shoppers and traders. LCP is investing £8m in the scheme, and much careful planning has been done to ensure that, by the millennium, 'visitors to the Wulfrun Centre have a better, safer and more attractive shopping environment.'

First of all, there will be more retail space. The new development will make available an extra 3,000 square feet, and even before work commenced the plans had aroused a tremendous amount of interest amongst potential new occupants; the first store to snap up a spot was the toy shop chain The Entertainer, which was immensely impressed with LCP's proposals, and many other major retailers have followed suit.

In addition there will be the Metro Line, linking the heart of Wolverhampton to Birmingham which was completed in 1999. The terminus station in Wolverhampton is situated on the Centre's doorstep and will help to bring a whole new generation of shoppers to the Wulfrun Centre.

Above: *A picture dating from October 1968.* **Left:** *The Centre in December 1970.*

And the appearance of the Wulfrun Centre will be totally transformed. The open-air malls will be covered with glazed rooflights, as will Wulfrun Square, making the Centre a cheerful, comfortable and welcoming place no matter what the weather. Outside, there will be alterations to the facade and new entrance canopies will be erected, as well as the imposing new entrance facing Dudley Street. The Bell Street end will be reconfigured and will include new kiosks on each side of the bridge link to the centre. Inside, the narrow curved mall will be realigned to form a focal point, and the central circus area and Wulfrun Square will become another focal point featuring a new mall cafe and craft barrows. New seating areas will be provided, and there will be new public toilets incorporating facilities for the disabled and for mother and baby. In short, the new Wulfrun Centre will have everything one could wish for, combining shopping and entertainment under one glass roof with easy access to both public transport and ample car parking.

It is an ambitious scheme, but one which Wolverhampton, an established market town with an estimated shopping population of 500,000, is ready for. When the new Wulfrun Centre is completed in time for the next century, shopping in Wolverhampton will once again become an exciting and stimulating experience, as it was when the Wulfrun Centre was first opened in the 60s. So Wolverhampton will launch into the new millennium as a strong, thriving shopping and entertainment centre, and the new Wulfrun Centre will be at its very heart.

Above and left: Two pictures dating from 1970.
Below: An artist's impression of how the New Wulfrun Square will be after refurbishments.

The family firm that's happy for its customers to walk all over it

Wolverhampton Market has been a testing-ground for many business ventures; some have succeeded and some have not, but one business which began in Wolverhampton Market in the early 1900s and which has very definitely stood the test of time is J Potts & Son.

The market was situated where the Civic Centre now stands when Joseph Potts first took a stall and began selling china and glassware. Joseph and his wife Beatrice lived in a house in St Peters Square, close to the market. Trading beneath a large sign which announced proudly: J Potts, English China Stores - Open Daily, Joseph's stall managed to build up a steady trade. In the late 1930s it was arranged that one of his daughters took part in running the stall, continuing to sell china and glassware while Joseph himself set off in a new direction, moving into carpets, rugs and linoleum. Ernest Gordon Potts joined his father Joseph in developing the business now known as J Potts & Son.

Sadly in 1941 Joseph Potts died, leaving Ernest the family business. That same year Ernest married Florence but unfortunately left to go to war. During these years his mother, Beatrice, kept the business running until his return. After the war, Ernest, supported by his wife Florence, developed the business. Ernest would travel by train to the factories where he would collect the rugs and lino which he had chosen and take them back to Wolverhampton with him. The goods would then be delivered by hand cart.

The concept of fitted carpets was introduced and quickly became popular, offering as it did the practical advantage of improved insulation against draughts creeping up through the floorboards, as well as the feeling of luxury that wall-to-wall carpeting brings. The business enjoyed increased trade as local households replaced their existing floor coverings with fitted carpets.

The firm's future as a family business was assured when Ernest's son Gordon joined. Their presence in the

market was maintained up until 1995; by that time they had four market stalls and two shops and specialised in fitted carpets, stocking all the famous, quality brands including Axminster and Wilton.

In November 1996 Ernest retired leaving Gordon to run J Potts & Son from the School Street shop. Unfortunately the shop suffered an abrupt fate in the summer of 1998. It was one of nine shops constructed beneath a council owned multi storey car park which had been built in 1965 to provide parking for 535 cars. During safety checks conducted by the Council in 1998, cracks were discovered in the reinforced concrete building, and engineering experts advised that urgent structural repairs

Above: Beatrice Potts and Ernest Potts selling coronation tablecloths in 1953.
Top: The original market stall.

were required to make the building safe. The announcement came as a great shock to J Potts & Son and the other traders who were affected, and because of the safety implications demolition was scheduled to commence as soon as possible, giving them no time to find alternative accommodation. J Potts & Son has now obtained new premises in Salop Street, which it is hoped will be opening early in February 1999.

With the fourth generation of the family - Jonathan Potts now joining his father, Gordon - the firm continues to provide the same excellent service which its customers have come to expect. Currently specialising in fitted carpets and cushion flooring, it maintains an extensive and up-to-date range of stock which will give local householders an opportunity to examine the full range of floor coverings and make their selection from amongst the best products available within their own particular price range. Many of these customers are themselves the children and grandchildren of Joseph Potts' first

market customers almost a century ago; the family firm owes its success, above all, to the good trading relationships which it has built up with its customers through the generations.

Above: Ernest Potts and Florence Potts in the 1970s.
Below: The family today. From left to right: Patricia, Jonathan, Gordon, Ernest, Florence and Joanna.

Success 'charted' for well over a century

with the firm to became a partner in 1903, leaving in 1906 to join Deloittes.

Robert Hope Johnston, an expert in tax avoidance, was a partner between 1909 and 1928, and while he was there John William Molineaux (1918) and Ralph Legge (1927) also became partners. By 1928 the firm had returned to Queen Street and was practising under the name of Muras & Co.

Teddy Cowin was appointed in 1934 and became infamous for press-ganging Articled Clerks into playing for Wombourne Hockey Club on Saturday afternoons; the firm's hockey interest was strengthened when John Holloway, a County player, joined them after John William Molineaux's death in 1947, subsequently becoming a partner in 1949.

Ralph Legge died in 1951, aged 49, and when Teddy Cowin died the two remaining partners were John Holloway and Graham Wycherley, who has been with the firm since 1945, becoming a partner in 1952 at the age of 23.

Hatton & Muras set up in business as one of the town's first firms of Chartered Accountants at 50 Queen Street, Wolverhampton in 1880. This was the year in which the Royal Charter was granted to the Institute of Chartered Accountants, of which Robert Muras was one of the founder members, a privilege for which he paid the princely sum of 10 guineas.

Robert Muras' partner, Thomas Strange Hatton, was Burgess's Auditor of Wolverhampton or, in today's terminology, District Auditor, and was also the founder of, and for 38 years Secretary to, the Bilston and District Provident Society. He died in 1888 and Robert Muras continued to practise under the name of Hatton & Muras, moving to 83 Darlington Street in 1891, where he was joined by Nelson George Harries in 1895. It was with Harries that the eminent Sir Gilbert Garnsey, acclaimed by the Press as 'the wizard of figures', had served his Articles.

During this period the firm was the subject of an article in the publication 'Accountancy': they would visit their clients in a van into which there had been built a machine which resembled a giant cash register, on which accounting information could be analysed. In addition to this forerunner of the computer, the firm also acquired a messy liquid photocopier, believed to be the first of its kind in Wolverhampton.

On 1st April 1963 the firm of Muras & Co amalgamated with Baker, Jones & Co to form Muras Baker Jones & Co. Laurence Jones was reputed to be the

Sir Gilbert Garnsey was regarded as the outstanding accountant of the day, but was lured away from Muras & Harries by Price Waterhouse's offer of £2.0s.0d per week. Another of Harries' Articled Clerks, Francis Walford Higgison, did stay

*Top right: The 10 guinea receipt which Robert Muras received from the 'Institute of Chartered Accountants. **Above:** Robert Muras, the firm's founder member.*
***Right:** Alfred Baker and Laurence Jones with whom Muras & Co amalgamated in 1963.*

first to observe that Wolverhampton was the only town to build a ring road through the centre. Alfred Baker and Laurence Jones had practised from Waterloo Road since 1930, and subsequently from 338 Newhampton Road East. Two years later Muras Baker Jones & Co acquired TE Lowe & Co, a long-established firm which had begun practising as Incorporated Accountants, later to come under the auspices of the Institute of Chartered Accountants; Bob Bromley, the principal of that firm, became a partner of Muras Baker Jones & Co.

Further changes before the firm celebrated its centenary in 1980 included the move to Bradburn House, a new development in Art Street; the retirement of Messrs Jones, Baker and Bromley and the appointment to the partnership of John Whitehouse, Don Sheldon, Tony Elliott and Roger Quinton.

The firm celebrated its centenary with a dinner at Wolverhampton Racecourse, at which John Holloway retired as a partner and Gerry Peters and Martin Parker were appointed.

In the years since its centenary, the firm has seen the death in 1982 of Tony Elliott, the retirement of a number of partners and the appointment of Bob Cole, David Richardson and Dawn Baker, grand-daughter of Alfred.

The practice has recently moved to Regent House in Bath Avenue (a former home of the Inland Revenue) along with its associated companies Muras Management Services Limited and Muras Baker Jones Financial Services.

Muras Baker Jones & Co has seen many changes since 1880, a small but interesting one being the premium payable by an Articled Clerk for the privilege of training to become a Chartered Accountant. This was £30 in 1898, rose to 300 guineas then dropped to 150 guineas in the 40s and ceased in the 50s. Some things, however, have remained the same; the firm's active involvement with the Wolverhampton Society of Chartered Accountants since 1947, and with the Staffs, Salop and Wolverhampton District Society of Chartered Accountants since its inception in 1976. The firm has consistently been at the forefront of technology, though technology itself has come a long way since the firm's van was retired! Above all, the high standard of the professional services provided to its clients, upon which the practice's reputation has been built, has remained unaltered as the firm progresses towards its second centenary.

1880
Robert Muras, founder member of the Institute of Chartered Accountants, together with Thomas Strange Hatton, formed Hatton & Muras

1928
Name change to Muras & Co

1963
Muras & Co joined Baker, Jones & Co to become Muras Baker Jones & Co

1965
Muras Baker Jones & Co acquired TE Lowe & Co

1980
Celebrated their Centenary

1998
Moved to Regent House
Partners: Gerry Peters, Martin Parker, Bob Cole, David Richardson, Dawn Baker

*Above: Consultant: Graham Wycherley. **Right:** The current partners outside Regent House. From left to right: Dawn Baker, David Richardson, Gerry Peters, Bob Cole, Carole Pate (Director - Muras Management Services Ltd) and Martin Parker.*

'Men of affairs' since 1826

Most towns now and then have a local 'character' or two whom everybody loves to talk about, and one of Wolverhampton's 'characters', in the early 19th century, was William Manby, a local lawyer well-known for what some described as his 'overbearing' manner.

William Manby began practising law in 1826, and his practice has evolved into the Wolverhampton-based firm known today as Manby and Steward. Until 1920, the practice was run solely by the Manby family; then Frederick Steward, better known to his friends as 'Freddie', was invited to join the firm as a Partner. Originally from Worcester, Freddie had served articles with his great-uncle Samuel Southall, who held the distinction of being Town Clerk to the City of Worcester for over 49 years.

In 1923 the Manby line came to an end with the death of the last Mr Manby, and Freddie Steward carried on the practice, moving in the mid 1920s to 14 Waterloo Road, Wolverhampton and subsequently being appointed Clerk to the Staffordshire County Magistrates, a position which he was to hold for many years.

Frederick, who had himself been wounded during the first world war, was unfortunate enough to lose both his sons in action during the second world war. When peace returned, Freddie was joined by his nephew Tony Southall in 1946 and by Bob King, who had been his son Derek's best friend, the following year. Both Tony and Bob were made Partners in 1952, and Freddie remained Senior Partner

until his death in 1965.

The mid to late 1960s were a period of considerable expansion. Acting on behalf of Manders Plc, the firm had had an active involvement in the acquisition and development of the Mander Centre and Mander House complex, and in 1968 they became the first tenants of the prestigious Mander House, taking offices on the first floor.

Expansion continued in 1970 when Senior Partner John Thorneycroft established a practice at Bridgnorth, later taking over the old established firm of Cooper and Co. The Bridgnorth office of Manby and Steward still operates from Cooper and Co's old premises situated in the historic surroundings of 1 St Leonards Close.

The firm opened an office in Dudley in 1977; this moved to the prestigious Waterfront complex at Merry Hill in June 1992. The opening of a fourth branch office at Telford, Shropshire, in 1986, brought the number of towns benefitting from firm's services up to its present number.

Today, the fourteen Partners and their staff provide comprehensive legal services in ways undreamed of by their founder. The scope of in-house expertise is awesome; the Partners between them provide specialist expertise as Registrar to the Diocese of Lichfield, a director of the Staffordshire Building Society, two Deputy District Judges, and many erstwhile members of the legal department of the former Telford Development

Above: A recent brochure.
Top: John Thorneycroft - senior partner.

Corporation. The man in the street still tends to regard solicitors as being there primarily to help him buy and sell houses, but in the industrial and commercial heart of the Midlands, Manby and Steward's Corporate, Commercial Property and Litigation Departments are of vital importance to the locality they serve. As one would expect, the Bridgnorth office boasts a specialist in Agricultural Law - perhaps of all the work undertaken today this would have been the most familiar to William Manby in 1926. Areas of expertise virtually unknown then are now covered by the company's experts in legislation relating to families and to children. The firm has its own specialists to guide clients through the minefield of employment law and education law, while other Partners deal with the contentious fields of Planning and Compulsory Purchase. A specialist interest in Town Planning has also been developed.

A member of leading local organisations such as the Wolverhampton, Dudley and Shropshire Chambers of Commerce and Wolverhampton Enterprise Limited, Manby and Steward is also a founder member of LawNet, a computer-linked network of 70-plus substantial independent law firms throughout the UK and Ireland, with access to pooled resources on a wide range of matters.

LawNet is a progressive organisation dedicated to the 'Quality in Law' programme, and the excellence of the legal service provided by its members is assured by the LawNet Quality Standard, a statement of the best practice in the provision of legal services, which each member is committed to implement. The introduction of a mandatory standard, subject to audit, will be welcomed by Manby and Steward, a firm which has always placed great importance on providing the best possible service and on building and maintaining excellent relationships with its clients. The firm's experience and standing in the local community has been its strength for almost 175 years, and the Partners are determined to ensure that this remains the case.

THE FIRM HAS SPECIALISTS TO GUIDE CLIENTS THROUGH THE LEGAL MINEFIELDS

Above: The firm's previous Brierley Hill premises.

Jewellery for pleasure!

Justin Rudell, initially articled to a solicitor as a trainee lawyer, found the legal profession not to his liking. Britain was enjoying a return to prosperity in the years leading up to the second world war. He found temporary employment as a relief manager in the family hardware shops before setting up in the business which, via changes and improvements, he came to love and in which he enjoyed great success.

In the momentous year of 1938, he put £750 into his first shop at 97 Darlington Street in Wolverhampton. Quite a considerable amount, at a time when senior managers and professional men regarded £500 a year as a jolly good wage. His stock then was Fancy Goods, such as ornaments and giftware, and Leather Goods, such as purses, wallets, handbags and hand luggage. Discerning travellers then preferred leather cases which lasted a lifetime of handling by railway porters.

Justin Rudell, like so many patriotic people of his day, was a part time soldier in the Territorial Army. On the outbreak of war in 1939 he, and thousands of other well trained volunteers, were called to the colours. His young business was left in the hands of a Manageress. During this period, serving officers purchased ladies brooches in the form of anchors, regimental badges and pilot's wings which were proudly worn by the recipients.

On his return home, Justin Rudell set out to expand by purchasing the freehold of his own shop and that next door. Like others of his generation he never drove, so he was ferried to and from work by Etta, his wife. Once their son Tony started school, she was able to work with Justin and proved to be such 'a brilliant saleswoman' that she managed the shop

Right, both pictures:
The original premises pictured in the 1950s.

when he ran the Emu Brand factory inherited from his father. This company made electro-plated cigarette cases.

Justin's ambition to move into the jewellery business was realised in the exciting year of 1950. He invested the enormous sum of £1,000 in a small stock of diamond rings. A considerable gamble at a time when manufacturing purchase tax, added to the price, on luxury items was 125%. The post war hunger for beauty and pleasure ensured that the rings sold well and were all quickly replaced to establish the family policy of trading up and putting money in stock.

Justin's son Tony served his apprenticeship in Manchester at Ollivant and Botsford who were so

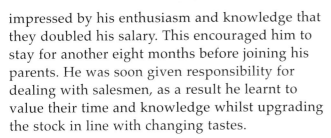

costing between £30 and £40 equivalent to £750 per ring today. In 1971 Tony's parents took a holiday to South Africa leaving him at the helm. During their trip, he negotiated the lease on the shop next door. They were so impressed with Tony's leadership qualities that he has remained in command ever since. In 1974 he became one of three founder members of the premier buying group in the country. There are now thirty two members enjoying the benefits of collective bargaining.

impressed by his enthusiasm and knowledge that they doubled his salary. This encouraged him to stay for another eight months before joining his parents. He was soon given responsibility for dealing with salesmen, as a result he learnt to value their time and knowledge whilst upgrading the stock in line with changing tastes.

In the 'Swinging Sixties' every Saturday saw the sale of some sixteen engagement rings each

Tony believes in offering a wide range of interesting items of good quality in an atmosphere where customers are greeted with a smile, shown a fine selection of jewellery watches and giftware and allowed the time to choose without pressure to buy. His joy in selling is matched by his enthusiasm for helping others through voluntary work with the Variety Club of Great Britain and other charities.

Above left: The founders, Justin and Etta Rudell at the firm's 40th anniversary celebrations in 1981.
Above right: Tony Rudell.
Left: The company's premises today.

Carol and Mercedes - two names for quality

The Mercedes Benz range, so the story goes, was named after Mr Benz's daughter Mercedes; so what could be more appropriate than that when Mr Hawkins acquired the Mercedes Benz dealership for the West Midlands in 1954, he decided to name his business after his own daughter Carolyn?

Wilf Hawkins was a keen Mercedes Benz enthusiast. A former solicitor, he bought a garage site in Oldbury, consisting of a repair shop and a petrol pump, in 1948, and later acquired extra land. As one of the first Mercedes Benz dealers in the country, he was responsible for supplying the Midlands, Shropshire, Worcestershire and Herefordshire. Wilf Hawkins was a firm believer in dealing with customers on a personal level, and this is a characteristic which has been shared by the subsequent owners of the business.

In 1968 Carol's Garage was bought by Harry Attwood, a well-respected local personality who owned a number of large motor trading companies in the area. Carol's Garage became Harry Attwood's flagship company, moving to the former Tractorvision factory in Wolverhampton in 1969.

Harry died in 1980, and the company changed hands a number of times before becoming part of the Clemence Automotive Group in 1988. Ever since then it has been managed by David Allen, whose involvement with Mercedes Benz goes back almost 30 years. David, like Harry Attwood and Wilf Hawkins before him, has ensured that the private, locally managed business has maintained the friendly atmosphere which has become its hallmark.

The current premises at Penn Road have undergone major redevelopment. The first phase, carried out in 1992, included a new service and parts centre and refurbishment of the used car showroom, with the second phase featuring an impressive new building to house the showroom and reception area. The showroom, spacious enough to display the entire range of Mercedes cars, has special backlighting designed to make it an attractive sight from the ring road, in an area which has been identified by Wolverhampton Council as a 'gateway site', one of the busiest roads into town.

Carol's long tradition of supplying top quality cars and light vans and servicing them to the highest standards has won it a loyal and stable customer base, and the company is proud that, with its new facilities, it is now equipped to continue this tradition into the millennium.

Above: The Garage today.
Top: Carol's Garage in the late 1950s.

From farm gate to dinner plate

FA Gill Ltd was founded on 26th January 1938 by Fred Albert Gill, a well established butcher based at 422 Dudley Road, Wolverhampton, and his son Fred Gill. Together they had recently opened a new slaughterhouse and shop at Parkfields Road.

Over sixty years later the Parkfields site has developed into an integrated plant, processing one percent of Britain's pigs and producing the pork for which the company is well known.

Now 90 years old, Mr Fred Gill still visits to keep an eye on the latest developments.

In the early years Gills built a reputation for quality pork sausages, and later in the 1970s, under the direction of Mr Christopher Gill, the company began to expand its distribution beyond Wolverhampton. Now making over 90 tonnes of sausage a week it is distributed to many customers across the country. Back in the days before the war, local deliveries had been been made in early Ford vans; now the company runs a large fleet of modern refrigerated vehicles. Mr Charles Gill is the fourth generation to be involved.

Very much a local company, its continued growth and success owes much to the dedicated local staff and the tried and trusted principles that were the foundation of the business in 1938.

Top: This picture dates from 1967. Charles Gill is the small boy on the front row. To his left are Christopher Gill, Fred Gill (junior) and FA Gill (senior).
Left: The Chilled Foods Exhibition in 1997 at the NEC.

The estate agents who can survey over sixty years of service to Wolverhampton

Wolverhampton people buying or selling houses in 1934 were fortunate in that they could benefit from the services of a new firm of estate agents: Sanders, Wright and Freeman, in King Street. This firm was set up by Harry Wright, whose father was the blast furnace foreman at the Round Oak Steel Works at Brierley Hill, in partnership with Raymond Sanders and Thomas Freeman, of Coventry and Leicester, to provide professional advice and services to local people and local and national institutions.

As commuter villages grew up around Wolverhampton, Sanders, Wright and Freeman found themselves selling properties over a larger and larger area. The change in commuting patterns and increased use of cars was indirectly responsible, too, for another change for the firm: having moved to Darlington Street during the Second World War, they then had to vacate these premises to make way for improvements to the Ring Road, and their next move took them to Lich Gates, Queen Square. They were to remain here until 1987, when larger premises became necessary to accommodate the increase in business, and at this point they moved to the prestigious offices in Waterloo Road which they still occupy, conveniently situated in the main commercial centre. Here, a separate Residential Department has been set up, managed by Dino Trubbianelli, a former pupil of Tettenhall College and an Associate of the firm.

Three generations of the family are now represented in this local family business. Harry, in his 88th year, assists with the day-to-day running of the business; his son Peter has been with the Company since 1956, and in 1983 Peter's son Michael also joined the business.

Peter Wright, FRICS, is currently Principal, and runs the Professional Valuation and commercial section; educated at Wolverhampton Grammar School and Aston University, he is a founder member and former Chairman of the Wolverhampton Auctioneers & Estate Agents Association, past Chairman of the Midlands Region of The National Homes Network of Independent Estate Agents and National Board Director. Michael, a former pupil of Regis School, Tettenhall, is an Associate, and manages the Residential Lettings section, an area which has seen the greatest growth in recent years with the Company now managing several hundred properties on behalf of landlords, many of whom now work abroad.

Now enjoying excellent local standing as Independent Estate Agents and Chartered Surveyors, the family firm of Sanders, Wright and Freeman is looking forward to a future of service to the community where the founder's family has had its roots for more than a century and a half.

*Above: The three generations of Wrights. From left to right: Michael, Harry and Peter. **Below:** The firm's offices in Waterloo Road, below left in 1910 and below as it is today.*

Combining the grandeur of the past with present day luxury

The Mount Hotel is situated off Mount Road, at the edge of Tettenhall Wood, where it enjoys an elevated and tranquil position, surrounded by gardens and ornamental woodland and well screened from the road. The main house was built as the residence of Charles Benjamin Mander; the Mander family owned a successful paint and varnish manufacturing business, and no expense was spared in the design of the interior of the house, where all the fittings, particularly the panelling and woodwork, are of the finest quality.

The original building dates back to 1865; it was extended in 1891, and the magnificent galleried ballroom, panelled in Canadian walnut with a fine Italian ceiling and a polished oak floor specially sprung for dancing, was added later.

The house was occupied by the Mander family until the death of Sir Charles Arthur Mander, Bart., in 1952, when it was sold by auction. Its new owner, Mr Dennis Norton, undertook to convert the property into a hotel, carefully preserving the style and character of the original interior. It was later purchased by Ind Coope, who extended the accommodation by adding a modern bedroom block. The hotel then became part of Embassy Hotels, and since 1990 has been part of the Jarvis Group.

Now a favourite conference venue, the Hotel has five conference rooms which can comfortably accommodate 200 delegates. Its 60 en suite guest rooms are equipped with all modern facilities and have full room service, and the Hotel can arrange babysitting to make its guests' stay as relaxing and enjoyable as possible. There are 'no smoking' rooms, ample free guest parking, and The Club Bar is an ideal place to unwind with friends. Dining in the Manders Restaurant is always a pleasurable experience, and with its high ceilings,

tasteful decor and fine views of the grounds from its leaded-light windows it provides diners with a pleasant atmosphere in which to enjoy their meal.

Throughout the hotel, the grandeur of the past is combined with present-day luxury; the stable block has been converted to a conference room and fourteen bedrooms, panelling and decorative woodwork abounds, and, looking at the imposing exterior, it is not too hard to imagine that the year is 1914, and David Lloyd George is about to draw up in his carriage to visit the Mander family.

Above: Lady Mander outside the Mount c1905.
Top: A picture dating from 1918, showing the Mander family entertaining David Lloyd George.

Providing a valuable service to local people

Having identified the need for a hospice in Wolverhampton, suitable premises were sought. With financial help from the National Society for Cancer Relief and from private individuals, institutions and Trusts, a building - Compton Hall, which dates back to the 1840s, was acquired and renovated, and the Duchess of Kent officially opened Compton Hospice on 9th November, 1982.

Compton Hospice cares for people suffering from cancer and other life-threatening illnesses. All services are provided free of charge and are available 24 hours a day, 365 days a year. The catchment area covers the populations of Wolverhampton, Dudley, Walsall, Sandwell and parts of Staffordshire and Shropshire - in all 1.5 million people.

The services provided include advice on symptom control and the treatment of pain, counselling of patients and relatives, a chaplaincy and welfare services. These services follow the patients wherever they are and include support for their family and friends during the illness and in bereavement.

A study centre provides a wide range of courses up to degree level for health professionals. Located in the suburbs of Wolverhampton, Compton Hospice has a 22 bedded in-patient Unit, a Day Care Centre open four days a week, nine clinical nurse specialists supporting over 230 patients in their homes and a lymphoedema service in partnership with Wolverhampton Hospital Trust. As this is the main office all the principal departments are based at this site. In Oldbury there is a thriving Day Care Centre which opens five days a week and is attended by over 80 patients per week from the Sandwell and Dudley areas. There are two clinical nurse specialists based at Wolverhampton New Cross Hospital, and at Little Bloxwich Day Hospice a contribution is regularly made to the specialist medical services.

It costs £3 million a year to provide the services at Compton Hospice and though it is partly funded by the six district Health Authorities within the catchment area, over £2 million still comes from the community at large and the sheer generosity of individuals, companies, support groups, friends, legacies and covenants, not to mention the hospice lottery and its charity shops.

Hospices have become an identified part of community life over the last 20, years and without the support of the public at large Compton Hospice would not be able to maintain and develop its services to the patients.

Big enough to cope, small enough to care

Hughes and Holmes was started in 1923 as a partnership when Mr and Mrs Hughes left their farm in Bishops Castle to venture into the industrial world. Their first business premises were at Snow Hill in Wolverhampton where the firm they founded remained for forty years.

The Hughes set up as tool suppliers and mill furnishers selling tools and equipment in an environment totally different to that of mixed farming in post Great War Britain.

Their business survived the debilitating era of the Depression in the early 1930s, so much so in fact, that a new shop was opened in Walsall just prior to the Second World War. Then as now their customers were tradesmen, both small independents and larger concerns. These customers, and the factories whose managers preferred the convenience of purchasing tools as needed to tying up money in their own stocks, have always been able to rely on Hughes and Holmes to supply their needs off the shelf.

The Second World War brought difficulties to small stock holders such as the Hughes business. Not only were the intermittent supplies of tools inadequate for their needs but Mr F C Hughes was conscripted into vital war work as a collier. His war time experiences working in a local mine followed by hours spent in the family business after exhausting shifts down the pit were not so unusual amongst civilians exempt from military service.

The post war era of burgeoning prosperity brought recovery and expansion to the family firm as it

extended its outlets and customer base to include local authorities and their schools as well as the general public in Walsall and Wolverhampton and at the newly acquired shop in Great Bridge. The business moved first in 1963 from Snow Hill to St Georges Parade, Wolverhampton and to Telford in 1973. The most recent move has been to the Key Industrial Park in Willenhall in 1998 allied with a change in policy to restrict sales to trade and local government clients.

As always customers of this well established firm of Engineers Merchants can rely on the knowledgeable staff and the immediate 'off the shelf' availability of the wide range of stock to meet their specialist and general needs. Currently stock control is being computerised to enhance efficiency and cost control.

Above: Cleveland Road Shop in the late 1960s.
Top: Snow Hill at the turn of the century.

An outing from Bob's Taxi's in Molineaux Street in the 1950s

Acknowledgments

Mr A Darby

Mr CJ Dowdall

Mr CA Eisenhofer

Mrs M Eisenhofer

Mr R Lloyd

Mrs M Tickell

Wolverhampton Archives and Local Studies

Wolverhampton Photographic Society

Thanks are also due to:

Peggy Burns who penned the editorial text and

Mike Kirke and Margaret Wakefield for their copywriting skills